PSYCHODYNAMIC-INTERPERSONAL THERAPY

SAGE was founded in 1965 by Sara Miller McCune to support the dissemination of usable knowledge by publishing innovative and high-quality research and teaching content. Today, we publish over 900 journals, including those of more than 400 learned societies, more than 800 new books per year, and a growing range of library products including archives, data, case studies, reports, and video. SAGE remains majority-owned by our founder, and after Sara's lifetime will become owned by a charitable trust that secures our continued independence.

Los Angeles | London | New Delhi | Singapore | Washington DC | Melbourne

PSYCHODYNAMIC-INTERPERSONAL THERAPY

A CONVERSATIONAL MODEL

MICHAEL BARKHAM, ELSE GUTHRIE
GILLIAN E HARDY AND FRANK MARGISON

Los Angeles | London | New Delhi
Singapore | Washington DC | Melbourne

Los Angeles | London | New Delhi
Singapore | Washington DC | Melbourne

SAGE Publications Ltd
1 Oliver's Yard
55 City Road
London EC1Y 1SP

SAGE Publications Inc.
2455 Teller Road
Thousand Oaks, California 91320

SAGE Publications India Pvt Ltd
B 1/I 1 Mohan Cooperative Industrial Area
Mathura Road
New Delhi 110 044

SAGE Publications Asia-Pacific Pte Ltd
3 Church Street
#10-04 Samsung Hub
Singapore 049483

© Michael Barkham, Else Guthrie, Gillian E. Hardy and Frank Margison 2017

First published 2017

Editor: Susannah Trefgarne
Editorial assistant: Edward Coats
Production editor: Rachel Burrows
Copyeditor: Kate Campbell
Proofreader: Neil Dowden
Indexer: Martin Hargreaves
Marketing manager: Camille Richmond
Cover design: Lisa Harper-Wells
Typeset by: C&M Digitals (P) Ltd, Chennai, India
Printed and bound by CPI Group (UK) Ltd,
Croydon, CR0 4YY

Library of Congress Control Number: 2016938549

British Library Cataloguing in Publication data

A catalogue record for this book is available from the British Library

ISBN 978-0-7619-5662-4
ISBN 978-0-7619-5663-1 (pbk)

At SAGE we take sustainability seriously. Most of our products are printed in the UK using FSC papers and boards. When we print overseas we ensure sustainable papers are used as measured by the PREPS grading system. We undertake an annual audit to monitor our sustainability.

This book is dedicated to the memory of Dr Robert F. Hobson MD with gratitude for his inspiring vision and teaching.

1920–1999

Contents

List of Tables

About the Authors

Michael Barkham is Professor of Clinical Psychology and Director of the Centre for Psychological Services Research at the University of Sheffield. He was Joint Editor of the *British Journal of Clinical Psychology* (2004—2011) and is a Fellow of the British Psychological Society. He was the international Vice-President for the UK chapter of the Society for Psychotherapy Research and, with colleagues, developed the family of CORE outcome measures widely used in practice-based evidence. He has led on several of the process-outcome studies in Sheffield and Leeds.

Else Guthrie is a Consultant in Psychological Medicine and Honorary Professor of Psychological Medicine and Medical Psychotherapy at the University of Manchester. She runs a busy liaison psychiatry service in Manchester and is a clinician and researcher. She has conducted many of the research studies on PI therapy in Manchester, including work on self-harm and persistent physical symptoms. Her other research interests include the interplay between physical and psychological disorders.

Gillian E. Hardy is Professor of Clinical Psychology and Director of the Clinical Psychology Unit at the University of Sheffield. She was Joint Editor of the *British Journal of Clinical Psychology* (2004–2011), and Associate Editor of the *British Journal of Medical Psychology* (2000–2005). She worked as a therapist/researcher on the Sheffield and Leeds research psychotherapy projects and has a particular interest in psychotherapy process research and attachment theory.

Frank Margison is a consultant psychiatrist in psychotherapy and general adult psychiatry working in Manchester. From 1978 he worked on the development of the Conversational Model of psychotherapy with Bob Hobson and led on developing teaching methods. His psychotherapy research apart from PI therapy has been in assessing client change using the CORE measure. He was UK Vice-President of the Society for Psychotherapy Research and was joint editor of the *British Journal of Medical Psychology*.

Preface

This book has been through several iterations prior to publication. We began with an attempt to write a definitive Handbook of Psychodynamic Interpersonal Therapy, a type of therapy also known as the Conversational Model. After a while we shifted focus and we have developed a much briefer book that focuses mainly on the very pragmatic aspects of doing therapy in this way. In many ways this goes back to the roots of the model in the very practical applications pioneered in the United Kingdom by Robert Hobson.

The opening chapter (Chapter 1) provides a brief introduction to how this model of psychotherapy developed, and links to other books on how it can be applied in the long-term therapy of serious, long-term personality difficulties (through the work of Russell Meares and colleagues in Australia). The chapter also introduces the theoretical basis of the model in outline.

Our original intention of summarising in detail the many research studies of this model has crystallised into two chapters (Chapters 2 and 3), the first of which summarise briefly the evidence that demonstrates that this approach is effective, and then a chapter on the many process research studies that together tell a story about how this approach may be effective.

The bulk of the book comprises six chapters (Chapters 4 to 9) that constitute a manual for a generic form of the Conversational Model. It is written to be suitable for beginners with little or no background in psychotherapy or counselling and can form the foundation for a teaching programme.

Chapters 4 to 6 cover introductory, intermediate and advanced skills. The introductory skills can stand alone as a generic approach to helping patients or clients to focus on important feelings, while the intermediate and advanced skills build incrementally to cover those skills needed to practise this model of therapy, especially in its briefer forms.

Chapters 7 to 9 develop the skills as they emerge in the beginning, middle and end of a therapy with some extended examples of an anonymised therapy based on actual sessions with Robert Hobson. These are not intended as exemplars of perfect practice, but rather as therapy conducted in real life, warts and all. Hobson emphasised the importance of learning from and acknowledging mistakes and we have tried to represent a realistic approach to conducting a form of therapy that is very easy to learn in its basics, but a life-long task to deliver at its best.

The book is also intended for those who already have a solid background in therapy or counselling who want to develop skills in this particular model. Some of the basics of how to start a session may seem redundant, but those aspects are arranged to lead logically into the fundamental skills and principles of the model.

For therapists who are already experienced in working this way, the book summarises not only the skills to be refreshed but also an introduction to how a programme can be developed to supervise and encourage the learning of others (Chapter 10) and finally Chapter 11 provides a brief overview of the life and work of Robert Hobson.

The book can be read sequentially and is designed to give an initial grounding in the model before the practice section, but it can equally be used initially as a practical manual, starting at Chapter 4, and the earlier theoretical basis reviewed later.

We have also included an adherence manual, where individual skills of PI therapy are summarised, anchored in a rating scale with examples to help use the manual in a consistent way. The scale can be used as part of training or in supervision when reviewing recordings of therapy sessions.

There are some additional resources and tools within the book, and more are available on the Psychodynamic Interpersonal Therapy website www.pit-sig.uk

Professor Michael Barkham (University of Sheffield)
Professor Else Guthrie (University of Manchester)
Professor Gillian E. Hardy (University of Sheffield)
Dr Frank Margison (University of Manchester)
April 2016

Acknowledgements

The whole of the development of this type of psychotherapy began with the work of the late Dr Robert (Bob) Hobson and Professor Russell Meares, and this book is our special thanks to them. Robert Hobson was active in much of the research cited here and was a principal investigator on several projects. We have worked closely with Russell Meares to make sure that the strand developed in the UK and the developments in Australia have kept synergistic links.

So many people have contributed to the development of this model of psychotherapy that it will be almost impossible to mention everyone, so we have tried to give credit to groups of people with named individuals who have contributed key developments.

Principal investigators of key research programmes in the development of the model

Professor Sir David Goldberg and the late Professor Peter Maguire were joint grant holders with Robert Hobson in the early definition of the model in the UK. Professor David A. Shapiro was a major figure and programme leader for the first process-outcome studies in Sheffield and we thank him for his involvement in an early draft of this book. Professor Francis Creed was programme lead on many of the early trials in Manchester.

International research collaboration with external programmes

Professors William B. Stiles, Robert Elliott and Marv Goldfried have worked extensively with the Sheffield programme and have contributed greatly to the elaboration of the way the therapy works. Many colleagues from the Society for Psychotherapy Research and other societies have contributed to our developing understanding. Professor Peter Henningsen led work to develop and test the model in a large multi-centre trial in Germany. Professors Wolfgang Herzog, Marco Rigatelli, Thomas Hyphantis and Dr Gaspare Palmieri have all been involved in significant European collaborations with the Manchester team.

Key research collaborators at the Universities of Sheffield and Leeds

We thank Dr Hannah Mackay who wrote an early compilation of process research studies. The late Professor Mike Startup with Professor Shapiro developed an early version of a chapter on adherence. Dr Graham Paley contributed work on approaches to training in the model. In addition, the following contributed to the delivery of the model in a range of process and outcome research studies: Dr Roxane Agnew-Davies, Alison Culverwell, Dr Susan Field, Professor Jenny Firth-Cozens, Dr Jeremy Halstead, Dr Heather Harper, the late Veronica Harrington, Professor Sue Llewelyn, Professor Anna Madill, Professor Glenys Parry, Ann Rees and Professor Shirley Reynolds.

Research colleagues in Manchester studies

We thank colleagues who have worked on the Manchester studies including Professors David Thompson, Bonnie Sibbald, Nick Read, Alistair Burns, Nav Kapur, Kevin Mackway-Jones and Caroline Chew-Graham, Drs Jane Hamilton, Joy Ratcliffe, Lasmi Fernandez, Graeme McGrath, Steve Reilly, Helen Barker, Jane Martin and Dan Beales. Stephanie Howlett has contributed not only to the work in Manchester, but also to developing the model for people with neurological presentations. Mrs Barbara Tomenson has been involved in the statistical analysis of many of the Manchester projects. Mrs Wendy Clarke has been responsible for the administrative support for many of the Manchester research studies and all the training courses we have run over the years. Without her support, very little would have been achieved.

Development of teaching methods and training in Manchester

We thank Madeline Osborn, Terry O'Dowd, Hazel Seidel, Susan Fairbairn and Steve Moss for their roles in developing the teaching materials, and many others who volunteered to play parts in the teaching videos and early development of role plays.

Malcolm Firth, Sarah Davenport, Roger Paxton, Dave Rhodes, Graham Paley, Jane Nicholson, Malcolm Judkins, Graeme McGrath and others developed teaching and evaluation, and clinical methods in other settings.

We are indebted to Jim Moorey and Eileen Brierley who set up and have been running training courses in PI therapy in Manchester for the last 20 years, and over that time have trained many hundreds of people. More recently, Richard Brown and Rebecca Hughes have also been involved in developing training in relation to a condensed form of PI therapy. Simon Heyland has been involved in developing and using the model in a primary care setting, and is currently playing a key role in the expansion of training in PI therapy. Clive Turpin and Rita Jordan have made an enormous contribution to training and using the model in the field of self harm.

We thank Professors Tony Roth and Steve Pilling, who have worked with us to develop a competency framework for psychodynamic-interpersonal therapy for people with persistent physical symptoms which can be downloaded from the University College of London website (www.ucl.ac.uk/CORE/).

Theoretical development of the model

Jim Moorey and Richard Brown have both made significant contributions to the theoretical basis of the model.

PIT Special Interest Group

We thank all the members of the PIT Special Interest Group which is geographically based in Manchester but covers the United Kingdom. We would like to pay special thanks to Simon Heyland and Sarah Bartlett who originally set up the group as well as Rebecca Hughes, Richard Brown, Mary Lewis, Kath Sykes, Wendy Macdonald, Sheena Grant, Liz Murphy, Graham Cooper and Clive Turpin.

Finally, Robert Hobson's son, Professor R. Peter Hobson, who has developed his own integration of therapist–patient relatedness from a psychoanalytic perspective (Hobson, 2016), has been an invaluable fellow traveller. We would like to give special thanks to Marjorie Hobson for her support over many years, and to Robert Hobson's wider family for support through the long gestation of this book.

PART I

THEORETICAL AND RESEARCH FOUNDATIONS

1

Psychodynamic-Interpersonal Therapy in Context

Introduction

This book contains the essential information about a model of therapy named psychodynamic-interpersonal therapy that has been developed over the last four decades. The book draws heavily on the extensive research base for psychodynamic-interpersonal (PI) therapy, which is summarised in Chapters 2 and 3. But the overall text is designed to be a compact summary and overview of this model of therapy that will enable practitioners, in conjunction with appropriate supervision and training, to implement PI therapy. Accordingly, Chapters 4 to 9 comprise a detailed manual to allow therapists to develop their skills and tools in practice. The model can be used as a development aid to existing skills in psychological practitioners, or can be used as a stand-alone model for experienced practitioners with more complex clients.

Psychodynamic-interpersonal therapy is relatively jargon-free and easy to learn as PI practitioners use everyday language rather than technical language to describe emotional experience. There is a strong emphasis upon 'knowing a person' as opposed to knowing about a person, coupled with the development of a strong therapeutic alliance. As feelings are re-experienced, they are linked to images, thoughts or prior memories, and then to key relationships. This process of linking feelings, thoughts, symbols and relationships occurs cyclically as the therapy develops and solutions are found and tested out both in the therapy and in the client's life.

The development of the model began in the 1960s when Robert (Bob) Hobson, a consultant psychotherapist, was working at the Bethlem Royal Hospital in London. Hobson ran a ward for patients with complex and enduring problems, many of whom would now be considered to have borderline personality disturbance. Hobson discovered that the traditional psychodynamic approach of that time was not helpful and, with his colleague Russell Meares, began formulating a new approach to treatment with much less emphasis upon psychodynamic interpretation and a far greater emphasis upon 'getting to know' the person and finding solutions to problems in the context of 'a conversation'.

Their essential idea was that the client's primary fundamental disturbance was a disruption or stunting of the ordinary experience of living. They viewed 'self' not as an isolated system but as part of a larger social organism. It follows from this theoretical position that the 'conversation of therapy' should involve a reciprocal shaping or picturing of the immediate central and emotional experience of the other, coupled with a re-working and re-processing of images, ideas and feeling states to form a more coherently operating self-system.

Hobson published his thoughts about a new approach to psychotherapy in a paper entitled 'Imagination and amplification in psychotherapy' (1971), and this was followed by a preliminary account of some of the features of the model in *The Pursuit of Intimacy* by Russell Meares (1977). Hobson then published a fuller account of the therapeutic approach in his book *Forms of Feeling: The Heart of Psychotherapy* (1985), by which time there was beginning to build a body of research on the model (see Chapters 2, 3 and 10).

Meares has further elaborated and developed the theoretical underpinning of the model (Meares, 1993, 2000). And a full exposition of his work with borderline personality disorder has been published recently (Meares, 2012a). The text is accompanied by a psychotherapeutic manual specifically for delivering the model for people with borderline personality disorder (Meares, 2012b). The model was originally known as the Conversational Model of therapy and this term is still used widely and interchangeably with the term psychodynamic-interpersonal therapy (abbreviated at times to PI therapy for convenience).[1]

The hallmarks of the model

This initial chapter introduces the four features that characterise the PI model of therapy. We briefly summarise them here and then amplify each of them in the subsequent sections.

1. *Conversation* – Psychodynamic-interpersonal therapy begins with the premise that personal difficulties can best be tackled within a relationship and that developing a personal relationship requires the therapist and client to 'discover a language that fits' (Hobson, 1985: 192); that is, to shape a common

---

[1] The term *psychodynamic-interpersonal therapy* is generally used as the name of this model, particularly in scientific discourse. The (or a) Conversational Model was the name preferred by Robert Hobson and Russell Meares. Throughout this book, the two names are used interchangeably.

'feeling language'. This is what Robert Hobson meant by a Conversational Model of psychotherapy. The therapist and patient engage in a creative process, a *conversation* in which shared understanding develops.

2. *Forms of feeling* – The notion of 'forms of feeling' is crucial to the PI model approach. When Hobson referred to feeling, he did not mean a faculty of emotion plus a faculty of cognition. Rather, he referred to a form of 'emotional knowing' or imaginative emotion related to an idea. This requires a different thought process to an intellectual way of thinking about problems and requires a form of creative imaginative or symbolic attitude which links together feeling states, symbols and 'analogues' to produce a sense of greater coherence. This type of analogical relationship is described by Meares as something providing a feeling of 'fit' or connectedness, showing the shape and proportions of something being described whilst not being an exact copy.

3. *Minute particulars* – Hobson used the term 'minute particulars' to refer to the ability of the therapist to pay especially close attention to the barely noticed nuances of a conversation so that by a painstaking series of adjustments, paying attention to minimal changes in inflection or gaze, the therapist starts to share an understanding of the other's inner state through a series of tentative hypotheses. Few other models of therapy focus so intently on the micro aspects of treatment.

4. *Research and practice* – The model has, from its inception, been grounded in a synergistic relationship between research and practice. Firstly, the PI model has a foundation in outcome research (see Chapter 2). This gives a clear answer to the question: Does it work? But, it is equally grounded in process research studying how people change in therapy – that is, research where the question is: How does it work? Our account of research on PI therapy takes the form of a developing story which progressively answers these key questions (see Chapter 3). In Chapter 10 we describe not only the research on learning this model of psychotherapy but also some suggestions about how process research methods can be used to enhance clinical practice by bringing in a different perspective of observation.

1. Conversation

A central tenet of the model is that the development of cohesion of the self depends upon a particular style of conversation, initially learned externally and then progressively internalised. This form of conversation is one that caregivers naturally adopt when bringing up young children (see Stern, 1985: 43). Some people are more naturally adept at this mode of relating than others. The process involves engaging with the child in an intimate form of 'emotional play'. It is this natural style of relating and capability to 'attune' to someone else that the model seeks to promote.

Hobson's strong belief was that it is the stories that matter – and how they are told. The skill of psychotherapists lies in their ability to learn and reflect back the language of the client and thereby create a 'mutual language' – a personal conversation. Hobson drew upon Wittgenstein's concept of 'language-games' (Hobson, 1985: 47). This is the notion that forms of language are particular and specific to shared activities of living and Hobson argued it was central to understanding the Conversational Model. The use of a form of words in one context may have a completely different meaning in another context. The important question is: 'What is this language doing within a particular situation?' (Hobson, 1985: 47).

The idea of 'conversation' as a principle is discussed further elsewhere in this book, but in considering the personal roots of the model developed by Hobson the actual conversations with colleagues over the years have had a powerful influence. In writing *Forms of Feeling*, he acknowledges that there is an inevitable bias towards the ideas that have arisen in conversations with friends. Two contributors to the idea of 'conversation' as part of the core of psychotherapy have been Russell Meares, who gives his own account of the Conversational Model elsewhere (see Meares, 2012a), and Miller Mair (1989).

Russell Meares, in his subsequent work on child development and the idea of the 'secret' as part of the development of a sense of a separate self, has carried forward the ideas of the Conversational Model into specific theories related to infant development (Meares, 1993, 2000). Meares was also acutely aware of the risks of a therapist 'knowing too much' and hence invading the personal space of the other in a therapeutic conversation. In their work on 'The persecutory therapist' (1977), Meares and Hobson specified the characteristics of an anti-therapeutic conversation that has been crucial in developing a teachable model of psychotherapy.

The conversational and rhetorical aspects of conversation and the 'poetics of experience' have also been closely linked with Hobson's work. He begins the Introduction to *Forms of Feeling* (Hobson, 1985: xi) with a quotation from Wordsworth:

> The principal object, then, which I proposed to myself ... was to choose incidents and situations from common life, and to relate or describe them throughout, as far as was possible, in a selection of language really used by men; and at the same time throw over them a certain colouring of the imagination whereby ordinary things should be presented to the mind in an unusual way ... not standing on external testimony but carried alive into the heart by passion. (Preface to the *Lyrical Ballads*, 1805)

Robert Hobson draws extensively on quotations from literature, but in a series of discussions he worked with the late Miller Mair[2] (1989) in elaborating a 'poetics of experience'. Quoting George Eliot in *Middlemarch*, Miller Mair points out that to be a poet:

---

[2] The late Professor Miller Mair was a clinical psychologist who became Clinical Director of Crichton Royal Hospital in Dumfries and Galloway. He worked closely with Robert Hobson in a series of training workshops during the 1970s and 1980s. He focused on the use of conversation and metaphor, and introduced the idea of a 'community of selves' with an internal conversation. These ideas and the emphasis on the poetics of experience resonated closely with the work that was developing on the Conversational Model at that time.

is to have a soul so quick to discern that no shade of quality escapes it, and so quick to feel, that discernment is but a hand playing with finely-ordered variety on the chords of emotion – a soul in which knowledge passes instantaneously into feeling and feeling flashes back as a new organ of knowledge. (Mair, 1989: xi)

As Miller Mair reminds us, Eliot notes that 'one may have that condition by fits only' – moments in psychotherapy – but Miller Mair, from his background in personal construct psychology, is referring to the same core principle that Robert Hobson espoused above. The emphasis on poetics of language was fundamental to Robert Hobson's understanding of therapeutic language.

For the purposes of simplicity, Robert Hobson and Russell Meares both distinguished two basic forms of language in therapy. The first is the language used to talk about 'things' that Hobson referred to as 'jam-jar language', and the second is the language used to share personal experience, which Hobson termed 'feeling-language'. The former is language we use to describe being in the world. It is literal and discursive and unconnected to feeling. It is the language we would use to say: 'That is a jam-jar'. The latter is characterised by a sense of vitality, a feeling of connectedness and a sharing of emotional experience. Hobson referred to it also as 'the language of the heart'. It is the language we use when we are talking intimately with a friend, family member, partner, or to ourselves.

Russell Meares developed this concept further by referring to 'chronicles' or 'scripts' to describe language that involves a catalogue of problems or symptoms, disconnected from the inner world. And he referred to 'inner speech' when describing figurative or emotional language (Meares, 2012b: 39).

Robert Hobson argued that a personal conversation, promoted in therapy, involves the development of a 'feeling-language'. This form of language expresses, communicates and shares feeling that involves: a) an apprehension of, and staying with, immediate experiencing; and b) a process of discriminating, symbolising and ordering experiences, especially by creative expression in 'living symbols' (using figurative language and metaphor).

So, one of the main tasks of a therapist using PI therapy is to try to promote or facilitate and share a kind of 'feeling-language'; in other words, to try to know and connect 'with someone' in therapy rather than talk about their problems or emotions. It is common for people to use 'thing language' to describe their feelings – 'it's my depression back again' – and this should not be mistaken for 'feeling-language'. The important distinction is between talking *with* someone as a person rather than talking *about* some experience they have had.

The work of therapy also includes owning experiences (thoughts, wishes, feelings experienced in relation to persons) in a movement from passivity to activity. This is characterised by accepting responsibility for actions and acts which had previously been disclaimed as a way of avoiding conflict.

2. Forms of feeling

The terms 'feeling' and 'emotion' are often used interchangeably. But when Hobson refers to 'forms of feeling' he is talking about elaborations of presentational symbols – emotions that are connected to imaginative ideas – as a kind of emotional knowing. Staying with feelings in the 'here and now' in therapy often leads to images, ideas, previous experiences, dreams, memories or physical sensations. These presentational symbols or mental pictures are elaborated, shaped and processed, dissolved and re-combined to eventually produce a harmonious organization or 'fit'.

Symbols enable people to elaborate 'inner forms'; conceptions which can be modified, combined, re-combined in the process of thinking and solving problems. Figurative speech, which involves symbolic language and metaphor, has a sense of movement and direction: There is a sense of layered meanings and complex connections.

The model emphasises the use of metaphor as one important way of exploring creatively a relationship between hitherto unrelated 'terms'. It is the process of exploration between two people (therapist and client) and, hence, the re-combination of meanings to create a new understanding, which is key.

Hobson was very aware that this theoretical account, at first sight at least, can seem hard to grasp, and he preferred to demonstrate the ideas in action. When asked by a trainee for a recommendation about reading about depression, he might refer to Conrad's *Heart of Darkness* rather than a psychiatric paper, although he was very familiar with the technical language of psychiatry as shown in his MD thesis on the physical treatment for depression.

3. Minute particulars

This concept of the 'minute particulars' arises originally from William Blake; Hobson, (1985: 108) cites William Blake:

> ... he who would do good to another must do it in Minute Particulars: General Good is the plea of the scoundrel, hypocrite and flatterer, For Art and Science cannot exist but in minutely organized particulars (Jerusalem III, 55: 60–68)

A focus on the microscopic forms of therapy has been a crucial part of the psychodynamic-interpersonal model from its inception. Russell Meares, when training with Robert Hobson in the late 1960s, brought Hobson audio recordings of sessions of therapy with a young man whom he was struggling to help. Meares found he could not convey in sufficient detail to Hobson the struggles he was experiencing without audio recording the sessions. Hobson and Meares found that 'within the minute particulars of the therapeutic conversation, systems of destruction and moments of aliveness were present in microscopic form' (Meares, 2012a: 13). They found a great deal can happen within a very few minutes of a psychotherapy session. Hobson wrote: 'The important focus is *how* a conversation is developed in its minute particulars. Broad psychodynamic theories are all very well: indeed, inevitably, they guide what we observe. But any formulation of the problem that faces a unique person must emerge from the manner of this conversation, *here and now'* (Hobson, 1985: 165).

PI therapy stands apart from many other modalities in its focus on the 'micro' interactions of therapy as opposed to the 'meta' world of understanding. A crucial aspect of this process is listening. All therapists using any modality of therapy would say listening is important. However, when Hobson referred to listening he meant more than simply attending to what is conveyed. Rather, Hobson referred to 'an active process of perceiving and paying attention to a multitude of verbal and non-verbal cues and by an imaginative act, creating possible meanings which can be tried out and modified in a conversation, or dialogue, that aims at understanding' (1985: 208).

Therapy involves a progressive, ever-varying exchange of information conveyed by complex cycles of action and perception. The challenge for the therapist is to learn the 'language' of the client, which can only be accomplished by 'listening' to what he/she is communicating in speech, gesture and feeling. It is salutary to listen to or watch tapes of therapy and see the myriad different ways in which clients converse, only to realise that we miss most of these opportunities for conversation because we are not sufficiently attuned to what the client is trying to tell us.

Although the audio recording of therapy sessions is now commonplace, in the 1960s it was rare and many psychodynamic therapists were actively and theoretically opposed to such forms of monitoring. But, Hobson and Meares – in the same way that Carl Rogers and colleagues had done in counselling – were pioneers as they realised that it is only by replaying and reviewing recordings of therapy that therapists can improve their listening skills and begin to become aware of the *minute particulars* of therapy.

4. Research and practice

A key characteristic of PI therapy is the way it draws together research and practice as two faces of the same coin. Formal trials of whether a therapy is effective are an initial step in building a therapeutic approach, but we describe ways in which the detailed analysis of the process of change alters and updates the model itself, and also the practice of individual therapists. The methods used in teaching this model are similarly based on good research foundations. But beyond this, we also encourage those learning to practise this model to use research methods to increase their understanding of their own sessions as described in Chapter 10.

This self-reflexive approach to practice can be strengthened by regular review of progress in therapy. It is beyond the remit of this book to discuss this in detail, but there is a complementary relationship between evidence-based practice and practice-based evidence (Barkham and Margison, 2007; Margison et al., 2000). This complementarity suggests that practitioners gain from looking at their own practice and reviewing the progress of that therapy against benchmarks derived from other practitioners through using simple, well-established measures of therapeutic change.

Chapter 2 briefly summarises 30 years of research effort including evidence that PI therapy is effective in mood disorders (depression), in some psychosomatic disorders (irritable bowel syndrome and functional dyspepsia) and personality disorder (studies of borderline personality disorder). In addition, the model has also been shown to offer benefit to people who have not responded to other therapeutic approaches. Further, the PI model has been shown to be cost-effective in practice.

However, it is of limited benefit to show that a therapy works if we have no idea what might be leading to that change. There needs to be a theory of why a particular type of conversation can lead to change. We also want this model of therapy to be grounded in what therapists actually do. So, the outcome studies referred to above have been linked to qualitative and process studies from which we have distilled some key lessons about how change occurs. This work is summarised in Chapter 3 as part of an ongoing narrative about what makes psychotherapy effective.

We also report in Chapter 10 studies showing that the basics of the model can be learned quickly, that those skills persist in practice, that the training has a positive impact on therapists and that trained therapists have a distinctive style that maps onto the fundamental tenets of the model. In our view there is no purpose in developing a new therapy without the confidence that it is effective and that training can be provided that focuses on the key therapeutic skills as efficiently as possible.

The theoretical and personal foundations of psychodynamic-interpersonal therapy

Having set out the hallmarks of the psychodynamic-interpersonal model as they are realised in therapy, here we consider both the theoretical concepts that have contributed to the PI model and also the personal influences on Robert Hobson that helped shape the formation and development of the Conversational Model.

Hobson and Meares have been influenced by the ideas of Williams James (1842-1910) – an American philosopher and psychologist – and Hughlings Jackson (1835–1911) – a Yorkshire-born English neurologist – in relation to the idea of 'self' as being a form of a stream of consciousness. Self is understood to arise out of a relationship with others. The psychotherapist Harry Stack Sullivan (1892-1949) – an American psychoanalyst – argued that 'a personality can never be isolated from the complex of interpersonal relationships in which the person lives and has his being' (1940: 10). Sullivan's model has been very influential in building an explicitly interpersonal model of the person.

However, there are areas in which Sullivan also retains a model of the unconscious even though markedly different from that proposed by Freud. He saw the contents of passion and conflict in 'shifting and competing configurations composed of relations between the self and others, real and imagined' (Greenberg and Mitchell, 1983: 80). This assumption that the self is a property emerging in relationships (internal and external) underpins the psychodynamic-interpersonal model and other modern theories of psychotherapy, such as Cognitive Analytic Therapy (Ryle, 1990; Ryle and Kerr, 2002: 34–36). And both approaches draw explicitly on the work of Vygotsky (cf. Leiman, 1997; Stiles et al., 1997). For example, both models draw on the idea of a 'zone of proximal development' (ZPD; see Zonzi et al., 2014 for an example within PI therapy).

Vygotsky worked on cognitive development in children and described the ZPD as the 'distance between the actual developmental level … and the level of potential development as determined by problem solving under adult guidance, or in collaboration with more capable peers'. In working with adults, the model is more like collaborative learning with no sense of hierarchy (see Chapter 3 for applications of ZPD in PI therapy). In addition, in PI therapy we have developed the idea of working in collaborative peer groups to extend the ZPD of trainee therapists as well as of clients (see Chapter 10 section on role-play groups).

As is common in relational approaches, PI therapy pays particular attention to the infant's development within a relationship (Meares, 1993). It is widely recognised that the infant has an intrinsic need to relate. As Sullivan pointed out, there are 'needs for tenderness' beginning with the need for bodily contact, developing into a need for an audience, and later needs for competition, co-operation and compromise. Failure to satisfy these needs at the appropriate developmental point leads to 'loneliness'. Hobson echoes this theme with his distinction between the creative state of 'aloneness/togetherness' and the terrifying state of 'loneliness' (Hobson, 1974). The theoretical underpinning for this core state has been further developed by Meares (2012a) but the detail goes beyond the scope of this book.

A complementary view of the early need for relationship is derived from attachment theory (Mace and Margison, 1997). The process of therapy is seen as an attempt to invoke an actual relationship with the therapist which is stable and responsive but within which the attachment representations can be modified to allow alternative, less maladaptive, patterns of relationship to develop (Holmes, 1996). Identifying and working with these patterns of attachment is a key underpinning of psychodynamic-interpersonal therapy. A key idea in monitoring whether these crucial conditions are being met is to consider the degree of 'attunement' between therapist and client as described by Stern (1985). Attunement is a concept widely used in counselling to mean attending closely to another person's state of mind. Here we mean something closer to the sense in which Stern refers to attunement as a form of conversation between parent and infant. The caregiver apprehends the other's affective states and responds with behaviour that corresponds with the infant's affective state, and finally the infant perceives a connection between the caregiver's statement and his or her own emotional state. This may be verbal or could be in the form of vocalisation or non-verbal gesture leading to a state of affective attunement. Stern conceptualised these states as the foundation for recognising that inner states are shareable.

Between adults, the same emotional exchange can occur and this experience is crucial in PI therapy. In some cases a longer period of therapy may be needed, as the belief that emotional states can be shared or even experienced directly has never been developed. With reference to the practice of PI therapy, Stern's description of 'amodal properties' (Stern, 1985) are especially helpful as they describe textural properties of a conversation such as intensity, rhythm, shape and cadence which are part of the 'minute particulars' discussed earlier.

PI therapy also draws on Jungian principles and Robert Hobson acknowledged the particular importance of Jungian psychology in developing his ideas. Hobson's own basic training as a psychotherapist was in analytical psychology and there are many resonances of the Jungian tradition in his writing. He acknowledges the influence of Fordham (1979), in particular his work on the Self. But the most important links are with Jung himself, and particularly Jung's approach to the practical aspects of therapy.

A profound personal influence on Hobson was his personal meetings with Carl Jung during the 1950s. Although by then a senior analytical psychologist and President of the Society of Analytical Psychology, Hobson admits to being surprised by the simplicity of some of the core elements of Jung's actual clinical work. Hobson distilled these principles and incorporated them into his own model. Many casual observers pay most attention to Jung's work with archetypes and myth, which are, of course, important in their own right. However, the central elements that Hobson drew from his conversations with Jung have much in common with current models of brief therapy.

There are three that are particularly pertinent. First, Jung emphasised the importance of a 'symbolical attitude' even in the briefest therapies and this principle has clearly been carried forward in the centrality of metaphor in the Conversational Model, and hence PI therapy. Second, Jung also used the immediate present, the 'here and now', in a particular way which focused the session in a, sometimes, challenging way. And third, Hobson's central idea of the 'conversation' was drawn from Jung's concept of the 'dialectical meeting': thesis, antithesis and the synthesis embodied in the conversation itself.

For Hobson, this emphasis, drawn originally from Jung, has strong resonance with the ideas of Harry Stack Sullivan (1953). Sullivan developed Interpersonal Psychoanalysis. He saw the contents of passion and conflict in 'shifting and competing configurations composed of relations between the self and others, real and imagined' (Greenberg and Mitchell, 1983: 80). This approach, which underpins the original Conversational Model, is fundamentally dialogical. This assumption that the self is a property emerging in relationships (internal and external) underpins other modern theories of psychotherapy drawing on the work of Vygotsky and Bakhtin.

Core values

All of the elements of theory presented above are embedded in the notions of a conversation, as described by Hobson and Meares. Hobson also invoked some core values that need to be upheld by the psychotherapist. Hobson returns frequently to the theme that psychotherapy is about 'persons' involved in a mutual conversation. '[S]ix qualities of a personal relationship ... are at the heart of conversational therapy: it happens between experiencing subjects, it can only be known from "within", it is mutual, it involves aloneness-togetherness, its language is a disclosure of private "information", and it is shared "here and now"' (Hobson, 1985: 25). This approach is central to Hobson's approach to therapy. In those six qualities he sums up some of the key principles of practice that we will expand in the subsequent chapters of this book.

A key paper from Meares and Hobson (1997; 'The persecutory therapist') shows how even well-intentioned therapists can be experienced as damaging and so the model of psychotherapy developed here is explicit not just about what *should* occur in a therapy but also what is unhelpful. These unhelpful aspects prevent the development of a therapeutic conversation.

Psychodynamic-interpersonal therapy as an integrative model

Psychodynamic-interpersonal therapy, as the name implies, can be seen to draw on several traditions within psychotherapy and can be seen as an 'integrative' model (Margison, 2002; Martin and Margison, 2000). One particular aspect of integration that was developed alongside the research programme described later is the *assimilation model* (Stiles et al., 1990; see Chapter 3). This illustrates how different approaches by PI therapy and cognitive behaviour therapy (CBT) can both aim to increase the assimilation of problematic experiences. However, as described later, the way that assimilation occurs shows key differences between an integrative relational approach like PI therapy and other models of therapy. Integration suggests that the elements are part of one combined approach to theory and practice, as opposed to eclecticism, which draws ad hoc from several approaches in the approach to a particular case (Hollanders, 2000).

The diverse range of influences involved in PI therapy as an integrative model have been discussed elsewhere (see Margison, 2002). In addition to psychologists such as William James, Rogers' person-centred counselling, self-psychology of Kohut, systems theory and Bowlby's attachment theory, Robert Hobson was influenced by literary figures including Shakespeare, Wordsworth and Coleridge in his approach to developing a 'feeling language'. He was heavily influenced by philosophers, especially Wittgenstein on language games, Christian writers including Martin Buber on the 'I–Thou' relationship and phenomenology through Rollo May on the experience of the self. These influences are explored further in *Forms of Feeling*, especially in the Notes and Note on Sources (Hobson, 1985: 283–99) where the breadth of influence becomes apparent.

Conclusions

This chapter has outlined the main background to the development of the Conversational Model and subsequently this model of psychodynamic-interpersonal therapy. It has complex foundations but now represents a distinctive tradition within psychodynamic-interpersonal therapies. The psychodynamic tradition is represented in the detailed attention to shifting states of mind, the tendency to ward off painful or threatening experiences, the underlying drive to form attachments and in the focus on disturbances of the self.

The interpersonal aspects are seen in the fundamentally dialogical approach and the emphasis on repetitive relationship themes. Both of these are in a context that draws on an explicit focus on optimising the therapeutic relationship and facilitative conditions (Rogers, 1951). The model of psychotherapy has been heavily influenced by the research that we, and others, have carried out and this work is summarised in the next two chapters. We look at the evidence that this approach is effective and also at the evidence that supports our model of the change process.

2

The Efficacy and Effectiveness of Psychodynamic-Interpersonal Therapy: A 30-Year Overview

Introduction

Psychodynamic-interpersonal (PI) therapy, or the Conversational Model, as it was and still is known in Australia, has been rooted in an ethos of scientific enquiry. Robert (Bob) Hobson in the UK and Russell Meares in Australia were both determined, from its inception, that the model should be teachable, researchable and evidence-based. Scientific study of the model has been continuing for the past 30 years and covers not only outcome research but also studies on the process of therapy and how the model is taught and practised. It stands apart from other psychodynamic and relational models in terms of the strength, breadth and depth of research that has been undertaken.

This chapter provides a brief overview of the outcome literature on PI therapy. The work derives from two major research methods: trials, which test the *efficacy* of a treatment under optimal research conditions, and *effectiveness* research, where there is less rigour but the setting is more routine. However, equally important as showing that a therapy is effective is building an understanding as to how psychological therapies work and lead to client change. The body of research focusing on the change process in PI therapy is presented in Chapter 3.

The majority of evaluative studies that are discussed in this chapter involve randomised controlled/comparative trials of PI therapy – that is, efficacy studies. Randomisation involves the allocation of the client by chance to a particular treatment limb of a study. In other words, a client stands an equal chance of receiving one treatment or the other. Although there are difficulties when this kind of evaluative approach is applied to psychotherapy outcome, it remains the gold standard and the main basis upon which influential bodies make recommendations regarding the standing of treatments and whether they are viewed as front-line treatments for specific conditions.

In other circumstances, evaluative data may have been gathered in routine clinical settings, a research paradigm that has been referred to as practice-based evidence or practice-oriented research (e.g. Barkham and Margison, 2007; Castonguay et al., 2013). Research has also been carried out into teaching and training the model (see Chapter 10). Such work is also included in this chapter where it helps to build a more comprehensive evidence base of PI therapy.

One of the hallmarks of PI therapy is that it is transdiagnostic in its approach and is potentially of benefit to a wide variety of different conditions. However, the following sections about its evidence base are grouped according to the main symptoms or presenting problems for which it has been evaluated. Although some of these groupings include diagnostic categories (such as depression or borderline personality disorder), others focus on problem behaviours (such as self-harm) or patients who are high service users who may have several co-existing mental and physical health diagnoses.

Depression

The studies on depression have been carried out by the Sheffield–Leeds Psychotherapy Research Programme, which has spanned almost 40 years of work carried out at the University of Sheffield (Social and Applied Psychology Unit; 1977–1995), University of Leeds (Psychological Therapies Research Centre; 1995–2007), and again at the University of Sheffield (Centre for Psychological Services Research; 2007 onwards). The research programme was founded by David A. Shapiro in 1977 and carried forward across much of this time with Michael Barkham and Gillian E. Hardy – as well as with other colleagues – together with the long-term international collaboration of William B. Stiles (Miami University), Robert Elliott (Universities of Toledo and Strathclyde) and Marvin Goldfried (SUNY).

The Sheffield team adopted a research model that contrasted the Conversational Model (initially referred to as *exploratory* therapy before then being termed *psychodynamic-interpersonal* therapy) with a psychotherapy drawn from cognitive behavioural therapy (initially referred to as *prescriptive* therapy in early studies). A feature of the designs adopted by the Sheffield group was that the same therapist delivered both types of therapy. This model of crossing therapists with treatments, rather than having different therapists nested within each therapy, provides a control on non-specific therapy factors and effects. However, some would argue that it is not possible for the same therapist to offer two contrasting therapies to the same high standard. Accordingly, the designs described here makes it crucial that therapists show fidelity to the model – they must not only adhere to the model they are using at that time, but the therapies using these two approaches should be easy to differentiate. The issues surrounding adherence are described more fully in Startup and Shapiro (1993). However, the research team worked closely with Robert Hobson to ensure that the implementation of the Conversational Model was as close as possible to his understanding of the psychotherapy process.

Comparative outcome trials

A key impetus that set the research agenda for the Sheffield–Leeds programme was a meta-analysis of 143 outcome studies published between 1975 and 1979 in which two or more psychological treatments were compared with a control group (Shapiro and Shapiro, 1982). The central finding was that the mean effect size for treatment approached one standard deviation, meaning that approximately 84% of the control group scored below the average person in the treated group. The results also suggested that the relatively modest differences between treatment methods were largely independent of other factors and that outcome research, at that time, was not representative of clinical practice. Further, the article concluded that the most promising research design for outcome research lay in 'same experiment' data in which studies compared contrasting conditions within the same experiment or trial.

The substantive and methodological yield of this meta-analysis provided the rationale for a quartet of successive trials, all of which were designed to compare two therapies – psychodynamic-interpersonal (PI) and cognitive-behavioural (CB) – as representative of the range of clinical therapies practised in the UK and elsewhere. While the studies held the comparison between PI and CB therapies constant, they used differing durations of treatment sessions as a further comparison – two, eight and 16 sessions. The reasoning behind the contrasting durations was two-fold. First, from a research design perspective, any experiment (or study) relies on a contrast being made and in three of the studies the contrast used was eight versus 16 sessions. It might be that while there would be no difference between PI and CB therapies for one of these durations, differences might appear when delivered in the other duration. Second, there was beginning to be interest in devising and delivering cost-effective treatments and an awareness that duration was a key factor in the design and delivery of the psychological therapies.

The (first) Sheffield Psychotherapy Project (SPP1; Shapiro and Firth, 1987)

The (first) Sheffield Psychotherapy Project compared prescriptive (cognitive-behavioural) therapy with exploratory (psychodynamic-interpersonal) therapy within the same experiment and used a crossover design in which clients were randomised to either eight sessions of PI or CB therapy, and then after that they received eight sessions of the other therapy with the same therapist (hence the term crossover). This design controls for patient, therapist and common factors. The aim was to maximise the sensitivity of the design to any treatment differences that might exist and thereby address the claim that equivalence in outcomes are found because true differences are obscured by weak research design.

The study comprised 40 clients referred for depression who received eight sessions of either prescriptive or exploratory therapy followed by eight sessions of the alternate therapy. The two eight-session interventions were separated by an assessment. The results are presented in Table 2.1. The main outcome study showed a small advantage for prescriptive (CB) therapy. However, further analysis showed that the differential effectiveness of the two treatments was confined to one of the two main therapists who had better outcomes for prescriptive therapy whilst the other therapist showed equivalent outcomes. Interestingly, this was an early investigation of the phenomenon of therapist effects using a sample of just two main therapists whereas current studies of this phenomenon would utilise samples of over 100 therapists (see Saxon and Barkham, 2012).

Table 2.1 The (first) Sheffield Psychotherapy Project

Study	Summary of methods and results	Sample size	Implications for practice
Outcomes (Shapiro and Firth, 1987)	Clients received eight sessions of prescriptive (CB) therapy and eight sessions of exploratory (PI) therapy in a crossover design, with each client seeing the same therapist throughout. The results favoured CBT although this difference was of moderate extent. The outcome was largely unaffected by the order in which the two methods were offered.	40	PI and CB therapy had comparable effects with a slight advantage to CB therapy, with little obvious from the sequence of the two therapies.
Therapist effects (Shapiro et al., 1989)	One of the principal therapists was responsible for most of the reported advantage of prescriptive (CB) therapy over exploratory (PI) therapy (Shapiro et al., 1989).	40 (as above)	Therapist effects are an important factor even under carefully controlled conditions.
One-year follow-up (Shapiro and Firth-Cozens, 1990)	Clients completed outcome measures at two-year follow-up. At both group and individual levels, outcomes were very similar to those obtained at the completion of treatment.	31 (sub-sample of 40)	Improvements were well maintained after the sequence of PI and then CB therapy or vice versa.

Follow-up at one year showed good overall maintenance of treatment gains, but, of course, the two therapies could not be compared at follow-up as all clients had received *both* therapies, so any effect would be totally confounded (Shapiro and Firth-Cozens, 1990). Clients were generally non-specific about what elements of therapy had been most helpful, but where they could identify factors they were often the more general behavioural elements of relaxation and anxiety management rather than more complex cognitive techniques or PI-specific elements.

The Second Sheffield Psychotherapy Project (SPP2; Shapiro et al., 1994)

The larger Second Sheffield Psychotherapy Project (SPP2) employed a more complex design utilising five therapists and compared CB and PI therapies whilst also testing the impact of treatment length – eight or 16 sessions – and severity of depression – low, medium, high – on outcomes with a sample of 117 clients presenting with depression.

More specifically, it focused on questions of therapy approach – is CB therapy more effective and rapid in its effects than PI therapy when delivered by investigators having no prior allegiance to CB or PI therapies? And of therapy duration – is 16 sessions more effective than eight sessions? The effect of initial severity was also considered as a key predictor. A battery of standard nomothetic outcome measures was used that included the Beck Depression Inventory (BDI), Symptom Checklist-90-R (SCL-90-R), and the Inventory of Interpersonal Problems (IIP). The feature of nomothetic measures is that the items are standard and there are norms for the scores drawn from clinical and non-clinical populations. Hence, the score of a client can be located in terms of either a clinical or non-clinical population.

In addition, an idiographic change measure (personal questionnaire: PQ) was used which helped to differentiate the rate of change of different problems experienced within the overall depression diagnosis. A key feature of idiographic measures is that the items are derived from the client's personal experience. Hence, a client might describe their depression in terms of 'Feeling like I am in a black hole' and this is then the item that they rate. It provides a way of generating items with unique personal meaning to a client, which is why the name personal questionnaire is used. A number of process measures were taken after every session for use in subsequent analyses as described in the next chapter.

Overall, the study yielded slight but not robust advantages to CB therapy with only the BDI yielding a medium-size treatment effect against PI therapy and no evidence that either therapy delivered a difference in rate of change. Table 2.2 presents a summary of the results. There was some evidence that 16 sessions were more effective than eight sessions, but mainly for the severely depressed clients.

Table 2.2 The Second Sheffield Psychotherapy Project (SPP2) and National Health Service Collaborative Psychotherapy Project (CPP)

Study	Summary of methods and results	Sample size	Implications for practice
Outcomes (SPP2) (Shapiro et al., 1994)	Clients completed eight or 16 sessions of either CB or PI therapy. Each of five clinician-investigators treated clients in all four treatment conditions. On most measures, CB and PI therapy were equally effective, irrespective of the severity of depression or the duration of treatment.	117	For more severe depression there is a clear advantage for the 16-session therapy. Otherwise results are broadly similar after either eight or 16 sessions.
Follow-up (Shapiro et al., 1995)	At one-year follow-up, although gains were, in general, well maintained, only 29% of clients were asymptomatic on all three occasions of testing without recourse to further treatment.	104 (sub-sample of 117)	Gains from therapy were reasonably well maintained but a majority of clients still retained symptoms.
Outcomes (CPP) (Barkham et al., 1996)	Clients were randomly assigned to CB or PI therapy delivered in either eight or 16 sessions. Gains in both treatment approaches were approximately equivalent and were similar to those achieved in SPP2 when measured at the end of treatment. However, clients did not maintain their gains to the extent that the SPP2 clients did at three-month and one-year follow-up assessments.	36	The study supports the effectiveness of PI therapy in clinical settings, although there were advantages to 16-session length of therapy in this study.

At one-year follow-up, eight sessions of PI performed worse than eight sessions of CB and 16 sessions of PI or CB (Shapiro et al., 1995). This suggests that for more severe depression where there is a clear client preference for a PI approach, 16 sessions are more likely to be effective than eight sessions. Or, conversely, in conditions where a maximum of eight sessions is available, CB therapy would be preferable where depression is severe, although in practice most practitioners would be considering, or obtaining an opinion on, medication as an adjunct for the severest forms of depression (see Elkin et al., 1989).

A sub-group of clients had a Cluster C personality disorder (that is avoidant, obsessive-compulsive or dependent). There were enough clients in this cluster to warrant separate analysis, which showed that for Cluster C clients with severe depressive symptoms there was an advantage for CB therapy (Hardy et al., 1995b).

The NHS Collaborative Psychotherapy Project
(CPP; Barkham et al., 1996)

In the context of results from the Second Sheffield Psychotherapy Project, there was interest in the extent to which findings obtained in a university research clinic would generalise to routine practice settings. To test this, a smaller effectiveness trial was carried out in clinical settings across multiple sites to determine whether the outcome results could be generalised to NHS outpatients. A total of 36 clients and four NHS therapists across three sites took part.

Results showed that clients yielded high levels of improvement and equivalent to those achieved in the SPP2 research clinic but gains achieved at end of therapy were not maintained as well at one-year follow-up. However, the overall effectiveness was comparable to that shown in other effectiveness studies. There was no advantage of CB over PI therapy in this study. The results are summarised in Table 2.2.

The Two-plus-one Project (Barkham et al., 1999)

The consistent finding of only small differences between differing therapies led to the design of a trial that attempted to maximise the potential impact of technically specific treatment components by delivering a very brief intervention essentially comprising two sessions with a follow-up session. The major challenge was to deliver psychodynamic-interpersonal therapy in this format. To initially pilot this format, Robert Hobson carried out several single cases from which the model was then formalised.

This pilot work yielded two articles, one theoretical and one practical. Barkham (1989) presented five central components of the model used for the PI treatment in the two-plus-one study based on a detailed analysis of one of Hobson's cases: (1) focus on the client's affect; (2) identification of a focal issue; (3) personal meaning of dream content; (4) emphasis on the interpersonal process in the 'here and now'; and (5) identification of a narrative point of origin. The practical article – one of the pilot cases – presented a fascinating single case study using the two-plus-one model in which Robert Hobson treated a thunder phobic (Barkham and Hobson, 1989).

The resultant trial compared psychodynamic-interpersonal therapy with cognitive behaviour therapy delivered in two sessions (two-) one week apart followed by a third session (plus-one) three months later (Barkham et al., 1999). The rationale was to package these treatments to a plausible minimum in order to maximise their impact as a cost-efficient intervention in which technical specificity would be the most prominent component at an early stage prior to the cumulative effect of common factors, which had been seen as one explanation for broadly equivalent results between therapies. A total of 116 clients were randomly assigned to either PI or CB therapies and received treatment either immediately or after a short delay (enabling a controlled evaluation of the short-term impact of intervention).

This very brief treatment, albeit for subsyndromal depression, was effective. Client gains were greater in the CB than the PI treatment, but again any advantage was modest. A summary of the study is presented in Table 2.3.

Table 2.3 Two-plus-one Project

Study	Summary of methods and results	Sample size	Implications for practice
Two-plus-one (Barkham et al., 1999)	Clients with a range of subsyndromal depression received three therapy sessions: two sessions one week apart followed by a third session three months later. Approximately two-thirds of clients showed improvement. There were no significant differences between CB and PI therapy, but at one-year follow-up there was a significant advantage for CB therapy.	116	Brief therapies are effective for mild symptoms. Client preference may be a rational basis for treatment choice.

Dose–effect relations

While these four studies held the comparison between PI and CB therapies constant, they used differing numbers of treatment sessions considered as an independent variable: two, eight, and 16 sessions. Studies have looked at the dose–effect curve; that is how response varies with number of sessions (Barkham et al., 1996, 2002). The results from two, eight, and 16 sessions was aggregated and this suggested a greater degree of linearity than originally proposed by the work of Howard and colleagues (see Shapiro et al., 2003). In approximate terms, this means doubling the dose roughly doubles the effect, whereas earlier work from Howard and colleagues (Howard et al., 1986) suggested that extra sessions have proportionately less effect. However, these overall relationships conceal the more specific point that more severe depression responds differently and requires more sessions, especially in PI therapy.

Data comprised both nomothetic measures referenced against the general population, for example the Beck Depression Inventory (BDI) and idiographic questionnaires that reference internally, measuring improvement or worsening against how things were previously, for example the personal questionnaire (PQ). The extensive data set was used to investigate further detail about client change.

Also, the PQ data, which was completed weekly throughout treatment, showed broadly linear improvements. But, within that overall picture there were differences such as the quickest improvement being in the area of symptoms, followed by relationship difficulties, and then self-esteem being the slowest to change (Barkham et al., 1993).

Routine practice

Moving beyond the research clinic, data has been collected from routine practice settings in order to determine the effectiveness of PI therapy. One key study – Paley et al. (2008) – focused both on showing that the PI model could be taught to a broader group of professionals and that their outcomes would be equivalent to those reported in the literature.

Data from 62 clients were assessed having received a course of PI therapy (median = 16 sessions). The results were reported using the BDI-II and a more generic measure of psychological distress, the Clinical Outcomes in Routine Evaluation-Outcome Measure (CORE-OM; Barkham et al., 2001; Evans et al., 2002). In addition, the results were reported for the percentage of clients meeting the criteria of *reliable and clinically significant change*. This requires the change in a client's outcome score to: (a) make sufficient change for it to be considered reliable (understood to be greater than the inherent unreliability of the specific measure); and (b) for the post-therapy score to be located in the range of scores that represent a non-clinical population.

Reliable and clinically significant change was achieved by 34% of clients on the BDI-II and by 40% of clients on the CORE-OM. Clients with high pre-therapy levels of interpersonal problems had poorer outcomes. Benchmarking the results against both national and local comparative data showed that these results were less favourable than those obtained where PI had been used in efficacy trials, but were comparable with reports of other therapies, including CB therapy, in routine practice settings. The results show that PI therapy can yield acceptable clinical outcomes, comparable to CB therapy in a routine care setting.

Psychodynamic-interpersonal therapy for depression: summary and current context

In summary, across a programmatic series of research studies aimed to detect treatment differences between PI and CB therapy, findings consistently yielded broad equivalence between the two interventions even when the design was optimised to detect differences (for summaries, see Barkham et al., 2011). Where there were small advantages, they tended to favour CB therapy, especially in severe depression where there was a definite advantage for CB therapy over PI therapy when treatment length is restricted to eight sessions.

Where symptoms predominate and interpersonal problems are less salient there is a case for offering CB therapy first, with PI therapy as an alternate where clients do not respond well to a CB approach. The studies also support longer therapies for clients with Cluster C personality disorder, interpersonal problems or more severe overall symptoms. In service settings no differences were detected between the two therapies, but these studies were not optimised to pick up treatment differences in quite the same way as with the two Sheffield Psychotherapy Projects.

The series of Sheffield studies and the subsequent routine practice studies suggest that, for depression, there is very little difference between contrasting or differing treatment approaches. A similar outcome for depression has also been reported between counselling and CB therapy within the UK government's Improving Access to Psychological Therapies (IAPT; Layard et al., 2006) programme (Glover et al., 2010). Indeed, considerably larger differences exist in the outcomes of clients who do not complete a course of psychological treatment when compared with those who do complete a course. In other words, enabling clients to remain in therapy is probably the best way of ensuring the best outcome as opposed to pitting one therapy modality against another.

Chronic and complex conditions

Depression has often been the initial focus for testing new models or applications of the psychological therapies as evidenced by the history of CB therapy and also of the UK initiative regarding Improving Access to Psychological Therapy (IAPT). Although the prevalence and burden of depression is huge, there are presenting conditions that are generally viewed as more chronic and complex. Logically, therefore, it is both a stringent test of the therapy and also a necessity regarding wider applications that PI therapy is tested in these settings. Such conditions include the following: chronic and intractable functional bowel symptoms, chronic refractory depression and anxiety, deliberate self-harm, Alzheimer's disease and borderline personality disorder. Such disorders are all relatively chronic and unremitting rather than episodic. Correspondingly, they present a greater challenge to therapists and researchers alike and are the focus of the remaining sections in this chapter.

Much of the work reported here has been led by researchers at the University of Manchester and were led by psychiatrists and clinical psychologists who had been trained in psychodynamic-interpersonal therapy by Robert Hobson (Else Guthrie, Frank Margison and James Moorey). Francis Creed was the principal investigator for several of the projects. The chapter also covers work carried out by Russell Meares' group at the University of Sydney in New South Wales, Australia, using the Conversational Model with people with borderline personality disorder.

The Manchester outcome studies of PI therapy were mainly concerned with the therapeutic evaluation of the therapy in a naturalistic setting. The principal foci were on clinical outcomes and effectiveness. For this reason, the main analyses were conducted on an intention to treat basis. Participants were recruited from clinical populations and attempts were made to make the studies as clinically representative as possible. In addition, the Manchester studies addressed issues of cost-effectiveness with a view to evaluating the economic basis for the implementation of a systematic psychological therapy such as psychodynamic-interpersonal therapy with people with chronic and typically intractable disorders that place substantial demands upon the healthcare system.

Medically unexplained symptoms

The term medically unexplained symptoms (MUS) refers to physical symptoms from which people suffer that do not have an obvious explanation for their cause through structural pathology of bodily organs or body systems. Such symptoms are unexplained and an organic cause is rarely found. As symptoms become more severe, multiple and persistent there is an increasing association with emotional and psychological factors (Henningsen et al., 2011). The symptoms are real in that they are experienced in the body, and causal mechanisms are multiple including a mix of genetic, physiological and psychosocial factors, both past and present (Haustiner-Wiehle et al., 2011).

Data from the UK Department of Health indicate that MUS is the most costly diagnostic category of outpatients in the UK and the fourth most expensive category in primary care (Creed et al., 2011). Patients with severe and persistent symptoms are the most costly to the health service and the prognosis for this group is generally poor, without specific treatment.

There are five randomised controlled trials that have evaluated the effectiveness of PI therapy for patients with medically unexplained symptoms (see Table 2.4). Three have been conducted in Manchester and have focused upon patients with unexplained bowel symptoms, and two have been conducted in Germany with patients with mixed bodily complaints. Four of the studies focused upon patients with severe and persistent symptoms (Creed et al., 2003; Guthrie et al., 1991; Hamilton et al., 2000; Sattel et al., 2012), who had not responded to conventional treatments and who had not been helped by specialist medical care, whilst the fifth study involved patients in a primary care setting (Schaefert et al., 2013). These studies are presented here in chronological order.

Guthrie et al. (1991): The first study recruited 102 patients with severe and intractable irritable bowel syndrome. Patients were recruited consecutively from a gastrointestinal outpatient clinic and randomised either to brief PI therapy or supportive therapy. All patients had had intractable symptoms, which had failed to respond to conventional treatments. The PI group received one long initial session of therapy lasting up to three–four hours followed by six sessions of 45 minutes, spread over 12 weeks. Patients in the supportive limb were seen on five occasions for 30 minutes per session. The supportive sessions were used to control for the non-specific effects of therapy (for example, seeing someone on a regular basis, and being listened to and supported).

The outcome of the trial showed that patients who received PI therapy showed a significant reduction in both gut symptoms and psychological symptoms in comparison to the patients who received support. The improvement in outcome was maintained over 12 months. Ratings were carried out by gastroenterologists who remained blind to the treatment groups.

Hamilton et al. (2000): In the second study patients were recruited with severe and intractable functional dyspepsia (for example, patients with persistent

Table 2.4   Evaluations of PI therapy for patients with medically unexplained symptoms

Condition and Study	Design	Sample size	Outcome
Severe, intractable irritable bowel syndrome (Guthrie et al., 1991)	PI therapy versus Supportive therapy RCT	102	Greater improvement in IBS symptoms for patients who received PI therapy versus controls. Improvement maintained at 12 months.
Severe functional dyspepsia (Hamilton et al., 2000)	PI therapy versus Supportive therapy RCT	83	Greater improvement in upper gastrointestinal symptoms for patients who received PI therapy in comparison with controls. Improvement maintained at six-month follow-up.
Severe irritable bowel syndrome (Creed et al., 2003)	PI therapy versus paroxetine versus usual care Multi-centre RCT	257	Greater improvement in health function for patients who received PI therapy and paroxetine versus controls at one-year follow-up post-treatment. Greater savings in costs for PI therapy group versus usual care group through reductions in health-service use over 12 months post-treatment.
Multisomatoform disorder (Sattel et al., 2012)	PI therapy versus enhanced medical care Multi-centre RCT	221	Greater improvement in health status for patients who received PI therapy in comparison with controls at one-year follow-up. No effects on healthcare use.
MUS patients with persistent symptom for at least six months (Schaefert et al., 2013)	PI informed group therapy versus usual care. Cluster randomised RCT	304	Significant improvement in mental health status for treatment versus controls at 12 months after baseline. No difference in physical health status. Number of GP visits significantly reduced in treatment versus control group.

upper gastrointestinal complaints). Patients in this study were randomised to PI therapy versus supportive therapy. Patients who were randomised to the supportive therapy received exactly the same amount of time with a therapist and the therapy was again conducted over a 12-week period. The outcome showed that PI therapy was superior to the supportive condition both at the end of treatment and at follow-up six months later. As with the first study, assessment of patient improvement was carried out by gastroenterologists who were blind to the trial groups.

Creed et al. (2003): In the third trial, 257 patients with severe and persistent irritable bowel syndrome were randomised to 12 weeks of PI therapy, or treatment with an antidepressant or usual treatment. Detailed assessments of outcomes and costs were undertaken. Both PI therapy and antidepressant treatment resulted in significantly improved outcomes at 12 months post-treatment in relation to both physical and mental health. PI therapy, however, was also associated with a significant reduction in healthcare use in the 12 months post-treatment, compared with patients who received usual care. So not only did PI therapy achieve a better outcome than usual care, it also resulted in significant cost savings. The average savings per patient over a year were approximately £1,000 (≈$1,500/€1,250) at the time of publication and for patients with the most severe symptoms, cost savings were approximately £3,000 per annum per patient (≈$4,500/€3,750) (Creed et al., 2008). Significantly more patients who received psychotherapy in comparison with the other two groups were also able to come off incapacity benefits with a view to returning to work.

Of interest, patients in the above study who reported a history of childhood physical or sexual abuse had a particularly good outcome following psychotherapy (Creed et al., 2005), and also showed evidence of physiological change in pain threshold levels post-treatment (Guthrie et al., 2004a).

Sattel et al. (2012): The fourth study of PI therapy for patients with MUS was conducted in Germany and recruited patients with persistent multisomatoform disorder. This disorder is characterised by severe and disabling bodily symptoms of which pain is the most common symptom. The trial was a multi-centre trial conducted in six different centres in Germany. A total of 211 patients were recruited to the study and were randomised to either 12 weeks of PI therapy compared with three sessions of enhanced medical care; the best routine care that could be provided. Patients were followed up six months post-treatment. The main findings were that patients who received the PI therapy showed significantly greater improvement in physical and mental health function compared with the control group over the course of the study. This is an important study as it showed that the results from the English studies using the PI model could be generalised to other countries and other healthcare settings.

Schaefert et al. (2013): The final study discussed in this section was also conducted in Germany but recruited patients with MUS in a primary care setting. Patients in the intervention group received ten weekly group sessions of 90 minutes plus two booster meetings in the follow-up phase. The groups were run by a psychosomatic specialist and a GP, and were based upon a PI approach to treatment with an aim to improve interpersonal relationships both within and externally to the groups. Patients in the control limb received usual care.

A total of 306 patients were recruited to the study. The main results were that there was no difference between the two groups in terms of physical outcome at the end of the 12-month assessment period. However, the patients who received the PI informed group therapy reported significantly greater improvements in mental health status compared with controls, and also significant reductions in depression and anxiety. Patients who received group therapy also had significantly fewer family doctor (GP) visits over the 12-month assessment period than did the controls.

Overall these five studies demonstrate that PI therapy is an effective treatment for MUS. The trials had low drop-out rates, which meant that the therapy was acceptable to patients and people were able to engage with the therapeutic process. The benefits of treatment appeared to continue post-treatment in several of the studies, with some patients making further gains in the six to 12 months post-treatment. In the UK, PI therapy resulted in a reduction in healthcare use and substantial cost savings (Creed et al., 2003). The final study by Schaefert and colleagues (2013) showed promising results for a group-informed PI intervention in the primary care setting. This approach did not appear to have a similar impact on the physical aspect of functioning as the individual treatments that were delivered in the previous four studies, but did show positive impacts upon psychological health and healthcare utilisation. Overall, the evidence suggests that PI therapy is an effective and cost-effective approach for treatment of MUS with various presentations.

Self-harm

Guthrie et al. (2001): There has been one randomised controlled trial that has evaluated PI therapy as a treatment for self-harm. In this study 119 people who had presented to a UK Emergency Department after an episode of self-poisoning were randomised to four sessions of home-based PI therapy in comparison with usual treatment. The therapists in the study were mental health nurses who were trained to deliver PI therapy, but did not have any formal psychotherapy qualification or prior training. The therapy was delivered at home to increase engagement and compliance.

Over 70% of people who self-harm cite an interpersonal problem as the main precipitant of the self-harm episode, so there is a strong rationale for using an interpersonal therapy with this group of people (Bancroft et al., 1977). Participants who received the PI therapy had a significantly greater reduction in suicidal ideation at six-month-follow-up compared with those in the control group. They were much more satisfied with their treatment and much less likely to report further self-harm during the six-month follow-up period than participants who received usual care.

This study showed that nurses with good interpersonal skills can be trained to deliver PI therapy for self-harm and deliver this treatment effectively. Following this study, a PI service for self-harm was established in Manchester. Nurses in other hospitals such as Hull, in the East of the UK, and the Wirral in Merseyside, Northwest England have been trained in the model and have demonstrated good clinical outcomes with reductions in service use (NHS Confederation, 2009).

High utilisers of mental health services

As PI therapy is a transdiagnostic treatment, it can be used to treat people who present with complex, mixed mental health and physical problems. A small number of people with mental health problems have chronic problems that are difficult to treat and account for a disproportionate amount of healthcare costs. They may find it difficult to engage with services, be unable or unwilling to take medication, not respond to diagnostic specific therapies because they have complex needs, or drop out of psychological treatment before it is completed. Many also have risk issues and may self-harm frequently or present to services in acute states of distress. Very few studies have explored the benefits of psychotherapy for people with complex disorders and enduring symptoms, who are high service users. PI therapy, however, has been shown to produce significant benefits for this group of service users.

Guthrie et al. (1999a): A sample of 110 people with complex mental health problems, who had been in treatment with specialist mental health services for at least six months without improvement, were randomised to eight sessions of PI therapy versus usual care from their psychiatric team. Those participants who received PI therapy in comparison with controls reported a reduction in psychological symptoms, an improvement in health status and a reduction in healthcare costs during the six months post-treatment. Participants who received PI therapy required less in-patient treatment, and less medication, GP time and nurse practitioner time in the six months post-treatment than controls.

Participants in this study often had several co-morbid psychiatric diagnoses. The most common was depression but this often co-existed with other forms of anxiety disorders, substance misuse problems or personality disorder. PI therapy was particularly well placed to help people with these kinds of problems because of its transdiagnostic approach.

Borderline personality disorder

Borderline personality disorder is a serious mental health problem, with significant mortality and morbidity. Individuals who are diagnosed with this condition report difficulties with distressing and extreme states of mind, problems with making and sustaining relationships, self-harm and substance misuse. They tend to lead chaotic lives and frequently report unhappy, unstable childhood experiences including abuse and neglect. The series of studies reported here are naturalistic studies and not controlled trials. They have all been conducted at the University of Sydney by a team led by Professor Russell Meares.

Stevenson and Meares (1992): There have been two major evaluations of the Conversational Model of therapy (the original term used for the PI approach and further developed by Meares) for people with borderline personality disorder (BPD), the first of which was carried out in 1992. Treatment outcomes were reported for 30 clients with BPD, treated with the Conversational Model of therapy for 12 months with two sessions per week. These clients showed significant improvements in mental health function over the year and marked improvement on seven behavioural measures, which included self-harm behaviour, violence towards others, use of drugs (both prescribed and illegal) and number of hospital admissions.

The clients who received therapy were compared with a matched group of 30 clients with BPD who were referred to the same clinic, but where no therapist was available, and they remained on the waiting list for one year (Meares et al., 1999). In comparison with this matched group, the clients who received the Conversational Model of therapy showed significantly greater improvements in mental health function. In a further analysis of costs, the use of health are of the 30 patients treated with this form of therapy was examined for the year prior to treatment and the year post-treatment (Hall et al., 2001). This showed a saving of AU$670,000 compared with a cost of the psychotherapy of AU$130,000, giving a net saving of AU$540,000 or AU$18,000 per patient. Most of the cost savings were in terms of reductions in hospital admissions.

Korner et al. (2006): The second major study was carried out by the same group of researchers, using a controlled design, in which patients with borderline personality disorder received 12 months of therapy compared with wait list controls. A sample of 29 patients who received therapy were compared with 31 patients who waited for 12 months without therapy but continued during that time to receive ongoing mental care and crisis support. There were significant improvements in mental health status and a reduction in self-harm for the patients who received therapy in comparison with controls. There were also reductions in emergency presentations for the patients who received therapy in comparison with controls.

Korner et al. (2008): In a further extension of this study, the researchers went on to compare different lengths of treatment for borderline personality disorder. They compared two groups of patients, one group received one year of Conversational Model therapy and the other group received two years of therapy. They found that the patients who had longer treatment continued to make further gains during the second year of treatment in comparison to the patients who received 12 months' treatment, particularly in relation to depression.

As stated earlier, none of the above studies involving patients with borderline personality disorder were randomised controlled trials, so some caution is required in the interpretation of the results. However, they provide preliminary evidence for the value of the Conversational Model of therapy for people with borderline problems, and point to the potential cost savings that can be made by providing timely and appropriate treatment.

Other evaluations of psychodynamic-interpersonal therapy

Shaw and colleagues (2001): An evaluation was carried out of inexperienced therapists using the PI model with patients referred to an NHS psychotherapy

Table 2.5   Other evaluations of psychodynamic-interpersonal therapy

Study and condition	Design	Sample size	Outcome
Clients referred to an NHS psychotherapy unit treated by inexperienced therapists (Shaw et al., 2001)	RCT PI therapy versus wait list Pilot	40	Significant improvement in those who completed therapy (before and after). Non-significant trend towards improvement versus controls.
Alzheimer's disease (Burns et al., 2005)	RCT PI therapy versus usual care Pilot	40	No difference between treatment and control for patient outcome. Carer improvement PI therapy versus usual care.
Complex clients treated by primary care counsellors trained in PI therapy (Guthrie et al., 2004b)	Before-and-after evaluation	41	Significant improvement following treatment with PI therapy. Twenty clients showed clinically significant and reliable change.
PTSD sufferers with complex problems (Guthrie et al., 1999b)	Time-series analysis	3	Improvement in all three subjects

service. Clients were randomised to either psychotherapy or wait-list control. Significant improvement was demonstrated in those patients who completed therapy, and there was a non-significant trend towards greater improvement in the immediate treatment group in comparison to wait-list controls.

Burns and colleagues (2005): Burns et al. assessed whether PI therapy could benefit cognitive function and affective symptoms in patients with Alzheimer's disease. There was, however, no evidence of improvement on the main outcome measures although there was some reduction in carer burden.

Guthrie and colleagues (2004b): An evaluation was carried out on the effectiveness of PI therapy for common mental health problems in primary care in a before and after design. Primary care counsellors were trained in the model (see Chapter 10) and their treatment, using the model, was evaluated in 41 patients. The patients who they treated presented with a mix of complex mental problems including mixed anxiety and depression, self-harm, alcohol problems and past histories of abuse. There was a significant reduction in psychological symptoms over the course of the treatment and 20 of the patients underwent clinically significant improvement. This study again demonstrated that the PI approach can be useful in helping people who present with a range of co-morbid mental health problems due to its transdiagnostic approach.

Guthrie and colleagues (1999b): This study described how brief PI therapy was provided to three people who developed post-traumatic stress disorder after being involved in the Manchester bombing in 1996. All three showed significant reductions in PTSD symptoms.

Summary

There is a robust evidence base for PI therapy in relation to other psychodynamic or relational therapies. It has broad equivalence to cognitive behavioural therapy for the treatment of depression and it is also effective for patients who present mixed mental health symptoms, unexplained physical symptoms and self-harm. There is also support for its beneficial effects for people with borderline personality disorder. Work on the model has been carried out in the UK, Australia and Germany. Three separate studies have provided evidence that PI therapy is cost-effective and can result in major cost savings for healthcare services over time. Its transdiagnostic approach may make it particularly suited to treat individuals who present with complex and severe problems with mixed and varying presentations.

3

Client Change in Psychodynamic-Interpersonal Therapy

Introduction

In the previous chapter we showed that when psychodynamic-interpersonal (PI) therapy is compared with another active treatment, improvements are broadly equivalent, and that PI therapy is helpful for many clients. However, we know that not everyone is helped and that some therapists achieve better outcome results than others. So, understanding what happens within a therapy and not just the end result is vital in order to improve clients' experiences and outcomes, to train therapists better, and to make sure we are offering clients the most appropriate treatment. This type of research – process research – seeks to understand *what* is helpful (and unhelpful) about therapy, *why* it is helpful, *how* clients change and make use of therapy, *what* is important to clients about therapy and *how* they understand what helped them change. Even tentative answers to these questions enable trainers to focus their training and practitioners to improve their skills and be mindful of what they do and how they are in therapy. Process research gives us a way of observing what we are doing, how we do it and why.

In this chapter, we provide a brief overview of some key process research focusing on PI therapy. The research has primarily been carried out using data from Sheffield Psychotherapy Projects. To present the key results in an accessible format we have focused on the findings rather than the methods and used the authors of studies as subheadings to avoid multiple references within the text. A summary of the studies is provided in Table 3.1. The five main areas we address are: the actions of PI therapists; the views of clients; the core elements of PI therapy; therapist responsiveness; and the assimilation model. We summarise the key learning points throughout the chapter.

Table 3.1   Listing of themes, their components and associated research methods

Themes	Components	Research methods
• Actions of PI therapists	• Adherence	Observer ratings of therapy transcripts using the Sheffield Psychotherapy Rating Scale (SPRS; Shapiro and Startup, 1992)
	• Verbal response modes	Observer ratings of therapists' speech using the Verbal Response Taxonomy (Stiles et al., 1988)
	• Intentions	Therapist completed post-session questionnaire, Therapist Session Intentions (TSI; Stiles et al., 1996)
	• Focus of therapy	Observer ratings of therapy transcripts using the Coding System of Therapeutic Focus (CSTF; Goldfried et al., 1997)
• Clients' views of therapy	• Helpful events	Client post-session questionnaire, the Helpful Aspects of Therapy (HAT; Llewelyn et al., 1988). Observers coded HATs using the Functional Impacts of a Therapy Session Coding Scheme (FIT-CS; Goldfried et al., 1997)
	• Helpful and unhelpful events	Observers coded HATs using the Therapeutic Impact Analysis System (TICAS; Elliott, 1985)
	• Impact of therapy sessions	Client post-session questionnaire, the Session Impact Scale (SIS; Stiles, 1980)
		Observer ratings of negative and positive client speech (Mackay et al., 2002)
• Core elements of PI therapy	• Aspects of a feeling language	Verbal response mode ratings (see above)
		Qualitative analysis of therapist language during HAT identified significant events (Hardy et al., 1999)
	• The here and now	Intensive qualitative analysis of one helpful therapy event (Mackay et al., 1998)
	• Mutuality and relationships	Client and therapist completed post-session questionnaire, the Agnew Relationship Measure (ARM, Agnew-Davis et al., 1998)

Themes	Components	Research methods
	• Alliance ruptures and repairs	Quantitative comparison of outcomes using the ARM (see above) to identify patterns of alliance rupture and repair
	• Shared understanding	Discourse analysis of a single case (Mackay, et al., 1998)
	• Insight	Comprehensive process analysis of insight events identified by client completed Session Impact Scale (SIS; Stiles, 1980)
• Therapist responsiveness	• Interpersonal style	Analysis of patterns of client interpersonal style (Inventory of Interpersonal Problems, IIP, Hardy and Barkham, 1994), PI adherence ratings using the Sheffield Psychotherapy Rating Scale (SPRS; Shapiro and Startup, 1992), Therapist session intentions (TSI, Stiles et al., 1996)
	• Attachment styles	Qualitative analysis of attachment issues identified in transcripts of client identified helpful session events (HAT forms, see above)
	• Client expectations	Client completed Opinions about Psychological Problems (OPP, Pistrang and Barker, 1992) before treatment and the Treatment Credibility Form (TCI; Morrison and Shapiro, 1987) before and after the first therapy session
	• Personality disorders	Clients assessed before therapy using the Personality Disorders Examination (PDE, Loranger et al., 1994)
• Assimilation model	• Assimilation stages	See Table 3.2 for assimilation model
	• Movement through the assimilation stages	Problematic experiences identified in therapy transcripts, which were then coded using the Assimilation of Problematic Experiences Scale (APES; Stiles et al., 1990)

The actions of psychodynamic-interpersonal therapists

The first set of studies described below considers what PI sessions look like or, perhaps more appropriately, how they feel, and whether it is possible to distinguish this form of therapy from other therapies. These studies capture what therapists do, their style, their intentions and the focus of therapy sessions.

Adherence ratings

Shapiro and Startup (1992); Startup and Shapiro (1993): These studies show that therapists do indeed offer interventions that are consistent with the model of therapy they are practising and that they can *adhere* to the model. When independent observers rated PI and CB therapy sessions using a scale that focused on behaviours specific to each therapy, as well as some facilitating factors present in both (e.g. being empathic), almost all sessions were recognised as the appropriate treatment and the interventions used were overwhelmingly those appropriate to each model (i.e. PI or CB therapy).

Verbal response modes

Hardy and Shapiro (1985); Stiles et al. (1988); Stiles and Shapiro (1995): Another approach to describing the content of therapy uses more general therapeutic categories called *verbal response modes* (VRMs). These are general categories that describe the differing functions of speech, for example: disclosure, question, acknowledgement or reflection. Compared with CB therapists, PI therapists use more simple reflections, interpretations and exploratory reflection, which is what we would expect from the PI model. PI therapists also used more exploring and interpreting verbal exchanges or conversations than CB therapists.

Box 3.1   Response modes

PI therapists use more reflection – both simple reflection back and more complex reflection that goes beyond what the client actually said.

PI therapists also use more interpretation which, in this context, means making an educated guess about the other person's feelings.

Intentions

Stiles et al. (1989; 1996): In addition, two studies have focused on the intentions of the therapist – that is, why a therapist was saying particular things. They found CB therapists more often focused on reinforcing and encouraging change, clients' cognitions and behaviours, and getting information. By contrast, PI therapists paid attention to feelings, insight and client–therapist relationship problems.

Focus of therapy

Goldfried et al. (1997): In research centred on the *focus* of therapy, findings also supported the expected differences between CB and PI therapists. For example, PI therapy had a greater focus on interpersonal themes (within-session experiences and a client's past and current relationships) as well as emotional issues. By contrast, CB therapy focused more on external situations and the future.

Box 3.2   Focus of PI therapy

PI therapists focus on interpersonal themes (in session, in the past and in the external world) and emotional issues more than CB therapists.

So, these studies confirm that PI therapists offer a distinct therapy and use interventions specified in the treatment manual. They have a different focus to those using CB therapy and their intentions are firmly linked to the underlying principles of PI therapy.

Clients' views of therapy

While the previous section considered how therapists and independent observers saw PI therapists' actions, this section considers clients' views of therapy. There are two studies that address what clients found helpful or unhelpful in therapy. The first study found that clients tended to identify similar helpful events in both PI and CB therapy, whereas the second study found this was not always the case.

Helpful events

Goldfried et al. (1997): Written descriptions were taken of events described by 43 clients from the Second Sheffield Psychotherapy Project that were identified as being helpful after a therapy session. A framework was applied to the accounts that took account of therapeutic change principles thought to be common to all psychotherapies: awareness, corrective experiencing, therapeutic relationship and hope. They found that clients in both CB and PI therapy sessions most frequently reported the category of *awareness* (58% of CB sessions; 57% of PI sessions). This category was followed by the categories *corrective experiencing* (25% in both treatments), the *therapeutic relationship* (16% of CB; 11% of PI) and, least frequently, *hope* (11% of CB; 6% of PI). There were no significant differences between the frequencies with which each principle was reported in each group.

Box 3.3 Four key change principles

Despite therapists being very aware of *differences* between therapies, clients tend to see the impact of four key change principles as equally *common* features and do not stress the differences between therapies:

- Increased awareness
- Corrective emotional experiences
- The therapeutic relationship
- Hope

Helpful and unhelpful events

Llewelyn et al. (1988): A similar approach to investigating helpful events used another coding tool and found differences between the two contrasting therapies. Clients in the Sheffield studies were asked to write down what they found helpful and unhelpful after a therapy session and these independent observers then coded these accounts. Findings showed that some positive categories (*awareness* and *personal insight*) were more common in PI than CB therapy, but also that clients experienced some unhelpful impacts more often (*unwanted thoughts*, *misdirection* and *repetition*). By contrast, *reassurance* was more commonly experienced in CB than in PI therapy events.

Impact of therapy sessions

Stiles et al. (1994): In these studies clients from the Second Sheffield Psychotherapy Project completed a session impacts form (Stiles, 1980) after each therapy session. Clients rated PI therapy sessions as less *smooth* and less *problem focused* than CB therapy sessions.

Reynolds et al. (1996): Clients also reported more negative impacts early in PI therapy compared with CB therapy. Changes in impact over the course of the series of PI therapy sessions were significantly greater than those for CB therapy. For example, although initial client ratings of session smoothness, positive mood and therapeutic relationship were less positive for PI than for CB therapy, this difference was not significant by the end of therapy. This may reflect difficult early sessions in PI therapy, with an emphasis on an uncomfortable emotional focus, and this became smoother over time alongside a better client-therapist relationship. Problem-solving also showed a similar slow start in PI therapy with more change as time went on. By contrast, in CB therapy, problem-solving occurred similarly across sessions.

Mackay et al. (2002): Clients in PI therapy experienced significantly more negative emotions than clients in CB therapy. However, outcomes were *better* when associated with higher levels of negative emotions. The reverse was true for CB therapy, where clients experienced less negative emotions in the sessions and negative experiences were *not* linked to better outcomes.

Together these findings point to similarities and differences in client experiences. One important difference is the reporting of negative client experiences within PI therapy as contrasted with CB therapy, perhaps particularly in early sessions. From a clinical and indeed ethical viewpoint, such potentially aversive experiences need to be justified. As we will discuss later, these difficult earlier sessions may arise because clients are talking with therapists about previously inaccessible feelings and memories that other therapies do not bring into focus. This is consistent with clients experiencing PI sessions as deeper, as the negative feelings associated with more positive outcomes suggest that difficult material is being emotionally processed in the sessions.

Box 3.4   Impact of PI sessions

PI therapy is rated as less 'smooth' especially in the early sessions when clients experience difficulties, which have previously been partly warded off, coming into awareness.

Core elements of PI therapy and outcomes

In this section we look at four key elements of PI therapy that are associated with client outcomes. These are as follows: aspects of a feeling language (finding the right language that captures the client's experiences); experiencing in the here and now; the relationship between the client and therapist; and development of a shared understanding.

Aspects of a feeling language

Hobson emphasised some important aspects of the language used in the delivery of PI therapy. He talked about focusing on the 'minute particulars' of the therapeutic conversation. This is very hard to research because such small nuances are often missed in more global measures of therapy. However, there is some support from one study that demonstrated the importance of very small details.

Stiles et al. (1989): Differences had been found between the two main therapists in the first Sheffield Psychotherapy Project in the use of verbal response mode *forms* (i.e. the grammatical forms used for the utterances). They speculated that even something as simple as how the therapist acknowledges something from the client could have contributed to differences in the effectiveness of the different treatments. Therapist 1 tended to use the form 'OK' or 'Right' when acknowledging what the client said. In this system these are called *interpretations in the service of acknowledgement*. In contrast, Therapist 2 tended to use so-called *minimal encouragers* such as 'Mm-hm' and 'Yes'. The former style tended to close down ongoing communication whereas the latter tended to facilitate it. Therapist 1 was found to be less effective overall than Therapist 2 in PI treatments. Showing a direct link between these differences and outcome is, of course, a different matter. However, this study suggests that it is not only the intent of the communicative act that is important but also that the precise detail needs attention.

Box 3.5   Minute particulars [1]

Even minute differences in the therapist style may impact on the experience of the client and influence the outcome.

Hardy et al. (1999): Another approach has been to consider the language of the therapist during attachment-related events in PI therapy. Small sections of client and therapist interactions were examined showing how therapist responsiveness enabled client progress. Both the content and form of the therapists' language encouraged both exploration of clients' feelings and containment for the client.

Box 3.6   Minute particulars [2]

PI therapy is sensitive to minute changes in language and the precise choice of words within a shared 'feeling language' may encourage exploration but also containment.

The here and now

Mackay et al. (1998): An intensive analysis was carried out of one event in PI therapy that the client described as helpful. The client found it helpful because she was able to express her anger, something that usually she was unable to do. The primary mechanism that enabled the client to do this was the therapist encouraging the client the stay with her feelings that emerged during the session.

Rudkin et al. (2007): Therapy sessions were examined in two good outcome cases compared with two unchanged outcomes in PI therapies. Good outcome sessions were characterised by high levels of client moment-to-moment experiencing and the therapist and client working together to construct meaning.

Box 3.7   The here and now

Relational therapies such as PI need to focus on the experiencing of feelings, 'here and now' in the session.

Mutuality and relationships

Agnew-Davis et al. (1998); Raue et al. (1997); Stiles et al. (1998a, 2004): Hobson emphasised the centrality of the relationship between the client and therapist in promoting change. As with most therapies, the quality of the therapeutic relationship in PI therapy has been associated with outcome; the better the alliance the better the outcome. However, in the Sheffield studies, clients rated the quality of their relationship with their therapist generally lower in PI than in CB therapy. There was also greater improvement in the alliance over therapy in PI than CB therapy. A question we cannot yet answer is whether it is possible to stay with re-experiencing negative emotions as part of the focus whilst also developing the good early therapeutic alliance that is so important in brief therapies. Our suggestions based on other evidence would be that close attention to potential alliance ruptures and their repair would be crucial as discussed below.

Box 3.8   Centrality of the therapeutic relationship

The better the relationship between the client and the therapist the better the outcome.

Alliance ruptures and repairs

Stiles et al. (2004a): Clients experience more negative events in PI than CB therapy, particularly in the early sessions of therapy. This study developed these findings and considered 'ruptures' in the therapeutic relationship. Using a sessional measure of the alliance completed by clients, 17 clients were identified who experienced an event with a 'rupture and repair' of the alliance (11 PI and six CB therapy clients from the SPP2). The outcomes for these clients were better than for clients who had not experienced an alliance rupture at all. This finding fits with a key principle of PI therapy – the importance of working in the here and now within the client–therapist relationship.

Agnew et al. (1994): It is important to consider how therapists can best manage relationship ruptures. We studied two clients in detail using qualitative research methods, and developed a model of repair that included six stages: (1) acknowledgement; (2) negotiation; (3) exploration; (4) consensus and renegotiation; (5) enhanced exploration; and (6) closure. This model of repairing a rupture in the therapeutic alliance is a microcosm of the PI model as the alliance repair includes some of the key features of the PI model alongside one of its fundamental aims – for clients to develop new and different ways of being in relationships.

Box 3.9 Resolving ruptures

Alliance breaches occur in all models of therapy, but when they do occur they are linked to better outcomes when the alliance is repaired in the 'here and now' relationship.

Shared understanding

Madill and Barkham (1997): A discourse analytic approach was adopted to study PI therapy and indicated that problems addressed successfully in PI therapy tended to be 'understood as belonging to the client'. Changes in the ways in which the problems were described through the course of therapy showed a shift towards an external attribution of blame in the two successful cases studied. In the unsuccessful case, the client and therapist had different ideas as to 'the problem'; the client presented it in terms of her partner's behaviour, whereas the therapist located the problem as belonging to the client (for example, relating the problem to her jealousy and low self-esteem). The therapist stuck closely to the therapeutic model, but this did not help the client, as little consensus was reached regarding the nature of the client's problems by the end of therapy.

Box 3.10 Shared understanding

A shared understanding of the nature of the problem is crucial for change to be enabled.

Insight

Elliott et al. (1994); Kerr et al. (1992): The work on insight brings together the key aspects of PI therapy discussed so far: use of a feeling language, experiences of emotion and a strong therapeutic relationship. In these studies client insight occurred following therapists' interpretation of clients' recent difficulties, delivered firmly, persistently and in a manner that encouraged feedback from clients.

Elliott et al. (1994): In this study the general features of insight events across therapies were found to include the following: the client is involved in recurrent, ongoing relationship difficulties; the therapist's interpretations formulated the client's painful reaction as a problem to be addressed further, and as relevant to a general interpersonal conflict theme; and the client's first response was to agree. Features of insight events that were specific to PI therapy included: a core interpersonal theme was raised in an earlier session; the therapist made appropriate and evocative use of a key word; and the client experienced strong or painful emotion.

Kerr et al. (1992) found that PI therapists focused more on making interpersonal links, or hypotheses, than other types of links and the interpersonal links were related to improved self-esteem.

Box 3.11   Effective focus on core themes

Relational therapies need a combination of a collaborative approach and firmness in staying with the task focused on an interpersonal theme, often using a key word or phrase both to signal and to contain painful emotions.

In this final section we introduce two models that have been developed out of the Sheffield process research studies. These provide a framework for thinking about how we adapt therapy interventions for individual clients. The models are pan-theoretical, they are not specific to one therapy approach, but they can help the therapist think about why a particular approach may be helpful with a specific client. We introduce first the model of therapist responsiveness and then the assimilation model.

Therapist responsiveness

Part of being competent in PI therapy involves being responsive in the developing relationship with the client. The PI principles of negotiation and reciprocation and of 'aloneness-togetherness' require the therapist to be aware of and responsive to clients' needs and ways of interacting. 'Appropriate responsiveness' is used by Stiles et al. (1998b) to describe the behaviour of an experienced therapist responding appropriately to differing client requirements, needs, abilities and circumstances.

Box 3.12   Appropriate responsiveness

'Appropriate responsiveness' is characteristic of experienced therapists who can respond appropriately to different client needs.

Interpersonal style

Hardy et al. (1998c): Therapists' responsiveness to clients' interpersonal style were investigated, hypothesising that such responsiveness may be one reason why therapies produce equivalent outcome findings. It was hypothesised that clients' interpersonal styles would 'pull' therapists to respond differentially even within theoretically pure, manualised therapies. SPP2 clients were classified either as over-involved, under-involved, or balanced in their interpersonal relationship style. It was predicted that therapists would respond to the intense feelings of over-involved clients by using PI type interventions in both CB and PI therapies. In contrast, it was expected that under-involved clients would engage relatively slowly and therapists, therefore, would preferentially use cognitive strategies.

The results showed that therapists tended to use more affective and relationship-oriented interventions with over-involved clients, consistent with these clients' overriding concern about maintaining relationships. By contrast, therapists tended to use more cognitive treatment methods with under-involved clients consistent with these clients' more distant, cognitive approaches to relationships. This latter finding was significant only for CB therapy. This may be because therapists were able to use a greater range of interventions in CB than in PI therapy and still be considered to be 'in model'. PI procedures aimed at maintaining the therapeutic alliance and dealing with affect may be easily 'borrowed' by CB therapists as part of the collaborative approach, whereas addressing faulty cognitions and setting behavioural tasks are not easily woven into PI therapy.

Box 3.13   Awareness of client attachment style

Being aware of the client's attachment style is important as it evokes particular styles of response from the therapist.

Attachment styles

Hardy et al. (1999): To further understand the process of responsiveness, a qualitative study examining sections of therapy transcripts was conducted. The transcripts contained events that clients indicated had been the most helpful in the session. The researchers classified the clients' attachment style, attachment issues and therapist response to the identified attachment issues. Attachment issues tended to focus on three themes: (1) concerns about loss or rejection; (2) conflict and danger; and (3) the need for closeness or proximity. It was hypothesised that therapists' responses to clients' attachment issues would be mediated by the clients' attachment styles and this was confirmed. Therapists responded to clients with preoccupied attachment styles by using reflective interventions and to clients with dismissing styles by using interpretative interventions. This finding confirms that therapists can be pulled towards using particular styles of intervention in response to a client's attachment style.

Hardy and Barkham (1994): This study found that attachment style, mentioned earlier in this chapter, also impacted on work problems in clients from the Sheffield studies. The clients who were categorised as having an anxious-ambivalent attachment style reported high levels of anxiety about their work performance and work relationships. In contrast those clients with an avoidant style were more concerned about the long hours they worked and their non-work relationships.

Box 3.14   Therapists' responsive reactions

Therapists tend to use more reflective responses (understanding hypotheses) with clients who have an anxious attachment style and more interpretive responses (explanatory hypotheses) to clients with an avoidant attachment style.

Client expectations

Hardy et al. (1995a): It was found that the greater the client's expectations of treatment, both immediately before and immediately after their first session, the greater their improvements in therapy. This latter finding was significant only for clients who received the shorter of the two therapy lengths (eight rather than 16 sessions), although it applied regardless of therapy type. For clients who received 16 sessions of therapy, their expectations of treatment did not predict outcome either in the middle or at the end of therapy. This suggests that the influence of expectations on treatment outcome does not simply 'wash out', but that it is important in those therapies when time for engagement or renegotiating the therapeutic relationship is limited. Socialising clients to therapy roles and tasks, therefore, seems particularly useful when therapy is to be brief.

Box 3.15   Socialising the client about their role

When therapy is brief it is particularly important to socialise clients into the therapy roles and tasks as that predicts a better outcome.

Personality disorders

Hardy et al. (1995a, 1995b): It has also been found that clients' endorsement of treatment principles and diagnosis of a Cluster C personality disorder differentially predicted outcome. Cluster C personality disorders include dependent, avoidant and obsessive-compulsive disorders, which are the personality disorders most frequently associated with depression. In CB therapy, neither clients' endorsement of any treatment principles, nor a diagnosis of a personality disorder, predicted treatment outcome. In contrast, clients who indicated lower endorsement of either CB or PI treatment principles, or clients who had a diagnosis of a personality disorder, did less well in PI therapy compared with those clients who highly endorsed CB or PI treatment principles, or who had no personality disorder diagnosis.

Box 3.16   Impact of Cluster C personality disorder

Cluster C personality difficulty predicts a poorer outcome for PI therapy.

The former findings suggest that maximum benefit from psychotherapy would not be achieved by simply offering clients the therapy they preferred. What appears to be more important, at least for PI therapy, is how strongly the client endorses that particular treatment. This aptitude or knowledge enables clients to make better use of the therapy. In contrast, CB therapies teach clients the cognitive model at the outset of therapy. The impact of prior knowledge and preferences may thereby be reduced.

Box 3.17   Client endorsement

Strength of client endorsement of the model is important as it predicts outcome in PI therapy.

Hardy et al. (1995b): In addition, it has been found that the influence of a diagnosis of a personality disorder on treatment outcome was also dependent on the client's severity of depression. It appeared that outcome was poor only when clients were more severely depressed and had diagnoses of a personality disorder. This suggests that the impact of these two disorders may be interactive rather than additive. Also, it seems that brief PI therapy may present some difficulties for clients with this type of personality disorder. This may mean that the type of work done in PI therapy cannot be done in brief therapies with clients with such problems.

Assimilation model

Assimilation of problems

Stiles (2002); Stiles et al. (1990, 2004b): The assimilation model is a pan-theoretical model of change that conceptualises the process of change in therapy as being specific to particular *problematic experiences* as opposed to a change in the nature of the person as a whole. An important implication is that differing problematic experiences may be located at differing stages within the assimilation model as the changes relate to memories, wishes, feelings, attitudes or behaviours within an individual person. Such experiences are problematic because they comprise, for example, threatening or painful events or difficult or destructive relationships. The model proposes that positive change is reflected in clients following a regular developmental sequence of recognising, reformulating, understanding and eventually resolving problematic experiences. Subsequent articles have updated the model very slightly and we present in Table 3.2 what is now considered the accepted model although some of the research reported in this chapter used an earlier version.

Stiles et al. (1990): Effective targeting of treatment also depends, in part, on clients' presentation of their problems. The assimilation model describes how clients present and may resolve their problems and how therapists' interventions assist in this process. The assimilation model argues that clients describe their problems in a way that reflects the degree to which they have assimilated a problematic experience into their own schemata. Schemata here represent cognitive structures that provide meaning and, therefore, link together a person's experiences.

Stiles et al. (1992): The model proposes that, in successful psychotherapy of any kind, the client's problematic experiences become progressively assimilated within their schemata, moving through eight specific levels, described in Table 3.2. The sequence of levels was based on clients' descriptions of the impacts of helpful and unhelpful events in therapy (Elliott, 1985). The client's

Table 3.2 Assimilation stages

Level	Stage	Description
0	Warded off/dissociated	Content is unformed; client is unaware of the problem.
1	Unwanted thoughts/active avoidance	Content reflects emergence of thoughts associated with discomfort. Client prefers not to think about it; therapist or external circumstances raise topics.
2	Vague awareness/emergence	Client acknowledges the existence of a problematic experience and clearly describes uncomfortable associated thoughts but cannot formulate the problem clearly.
3	Problem statement/clarification	Content includes a clear statement of a problem, something that could be worked on.
4	Understanding/insight	The problematic experience is placed into a schema, formulated and understood with clear connective links.
5	Application/working through	The understanding is used to work on a problem; there is reference to specific problem-solving, although without complete success.
6	Problem solution/resourcefulness	Client achieves a successful solution to a specific problem.
7	Mastery/integration	Client successfully uses solutions in new situations; this generalising is largely automatic, not salient.

affective state (e.g. distress, as measured by standard symptom inventories) is most negative at Stage 2, when the problem is emerging and most positive at Stage 6, when the problem has just been solved.

Detert et al. (2006) compared the assimilation of problematic experiences in four good outcome cases versus four poor outcome cases of very brief psychotherapy (two sessions plus a follow-up) for mild depression. Half of the clients in each group received a brief version of PI therapy and half received a brief version of CB therapy. Results supported the theoretical expectation that reductions in the intensity of depressive symptoms were associated with higher levels of assimilation. There were no significant differences between the PI and CB treatments. All of the good outcome cases reached assimilation Level 4 (understanding/insight), whereas none of the poor outcome cases did so.

Box 3.18   Awareness of assimilation level

Awareness of the assimilation level of a client's problem is a good indicator both of progress in therapy and what aspects of the problem need to be addressed.

Movement through the assimilation stages

(Field et al., 1994; Hardy et al., 1998a; Rees et al., 2001; Shapiro et al., 1992; Stiles et al., 1991, 1992, 1994, 1997, 2006): These studies looked in depth at individual stages of assimilation to understand better the therapeutic processes that enable clients to move from one stage to another in PI therapy. Common themes in these analyses suggest that therapists are both firm and collaborative in helping clients assimilate problematic experiences. For example, in helping a client move from the assimilation stage of vague awareness to problem clarification, the therapist was challenging and directive, whilst accepting of the client's distress and active in developing shared language.

Shapiro et al. (1992); Stiles et al. (1992, 1997): The assimilation model also suggests that clients with poorly assimilated problems may do better in exploratory treatments such as PI therapy than in CB therapies. Therapists using PI therapies often consider the client's presenting complaints as reflecting experiences that are not yet accessible or are avoided (APES Levels 0 to 2). In these therapies, formulation of the problem and insight (APES Level 3 and 4) are often the therapeutic goals.

These results suggest that CB therapy better targets and effects change when the problem is relatively well defined. In contrast, PI therapy aims to uncover problems that are causing distress and upset but which initially the client is not able to describe clearly. For clients whose problems were relatively clear, this uncovering process may have felt unnecessary and perhaps not helpful, especially as therapy was time limited in the Sheffield projects. These studies also show the value of therapists actively helping clients clarify what is troubling them and then focusing interventions appropriately to resolving these difficulties.

Box 3.19   Matching interventions to assimilation level

PI therapy is effective when the client still has difficulty articulating the problem but experiences distress, whereas cognitive approaches may be preferable when the problem has already been clarified.

Summary

In this chapter we have used process studies to investigate a number of questions. Most of this research has come from the Sheffield studies, where therapy sessions were audio recorded and clients and therapists completed questionnaires after each session.

Together the studies suggest that it is important for therapists to be flexible and responsive to client needs, especially to the interpersonal or attachment issues that confront clients. In addition, as attachment theory would predict, clients did better in therapy if they were confident in their therapists. In particular, assimilation of problematic experiences seems to occur when therapists are firm, collaborative and challenging.

PI therapy appears to do best when the client is committed to a psychological therapy prior to therapy starting. So, for example, both clients' treatment preferences and degree of psychological orientation predicted outcome in PI therapy. These findings suggest therapists should socialise clients into the treatment process with clearer exposition of what to expect during sessions and a better explanation of how change may occur.

In addition, they should carefully assess clients' needs and formulate their problems so that therapy can both clarify and be targeted at key client problems. We have also seen that it is important for therapists to recognise the impact of clients' interpersonal histories on the treatment process itself, and on the ability of clients to maintain the gains they make in treatment.

Finally, important and distinctive elements of PI therapy have been found to focus on three main elements. First, finding the right language that captures the clients' experiences and is understood by both therapist and client is a central component of PI therapy (Hobson, 1985) and highlighted by a number of studies. Second, studies have linked change in therapy to the experiential element, the experiencing of feelings, and events in the here and now, of PI therapy. Finally, the centrality of the relationship between client and therapist is evident in many studies.

PART II

PRACTITIONER MANUAL

SECTION A: LEARNING THE SKILLS

4

Core Model and Introductory Psychodynamic-Interpersonal Skills

Introduction

This manual focuses upon the minute interactions between therapist and client. It gives beginners to psychotherapy some answers to the following questions: 'But what do I actually say now?'; 'What do I actually do?' For more experienced therapists, it may provide an opportunity for reflection upon not 'What do I say?' but 'How do I say?' something.

The model comprises three stages with 13 distinct but interlinked components or competencies (see Table 4.1 for a listing). Some of these components are generic to all psychotherapies but, when taken as a whole, they constitute a specific and definable model of therapy. The competencies are divided into the three stages according to the ease with which they can be learned and practised independently. In this chapter, following a brief description of the core components of the model, the Stage 1 competencies of the model are delineated. The Stage 2 and 3 competencies are described in the following two chapters – Chapters 5 and 6 respectively.

Once learnt, the competencies can be practised and refined, just as a musician practises scales. A key concept is that of deliberate practice formulated by Ericsson (see Ericsson and Lehmann, 1996) in which he proposed that people become experts by hour upon hour of very deliberate practice. Evidence suggests that this also applies to being a skilled therapist (for example,

Chow et al., 2015). It might be supposed that this phenomenon is just a reflection of a practitioner's cumulative caseload, making us all more skilled with age. However, deliberate practice is more about the time and work put into training outside the time spent with a client. That will invariably involve repeated self-scrutiny and self-monitoring of audio files or video recordings of therapy sessions; supervision; and individual rehearsal and practice for all therapists, regardless of their level of competency.

Table 4.1   The three competency stages and associated skills for psychodynamic-interpersonal therapy

Competency stage	Competencies	Components within competencies
Stage 1: **Introductory skills (4)**	**The four Stage 1 competencies:**	
	1.1 Statements	
	1.2 Picking up cues (4)	
		1.2.1 Verbal cues
		1.2.2 Vocal cues
		1.2.3 Non-verbal cues
		1.2.4 Cues in the therapist
	1.3 Negotiation	
	1.4 Understanding hypotheses	
Stage 2: **Intermediary skills (4)**	**The four Stage 2 competencies:**	
	2.1 Focusing on feelings (here and now)	
	2.2 Metaphor and living symbols	
	2.3 Language of mutuality ('I and we')	
	2.4 Linking hypotheses	
Stage 3: **Advanced skills (5)**	**The five Stage 3 competencies:**	
	3.1 Explanatory hypotheses	
	3.2 PI therapy rationale	
	3.3 Sequencing of intervention	
	3.4 Relating interpersonal change to therapy	
	3.5 Patterns in relationships	

This should not jeopardise the genuineness of the therapeutic relationship; rather it should enhance the therapist's ability to tune into the person he/she is 'being with'.

The manual itself has existed as an informal document and previous versions have been used in research studies. These earlier versions were written in collaboration with Robert Hobson, and this version also draws heavily upon his book *Forms of Feeling* (1985). This manual focuses upon using the model in a brief framework and is based upon our experience of using it in an intensity of one session per week, usually in a 16, 12, eight, four or three session (i.e. two-plus-one) format.

Russell Meares, who co-founded the model with Robert Hobson, has developed the model for use in a long-term and intensive format for clients with borderline personality states, where there is a greater emphasis on reparative work of the self and the development of a sense of coherence. Readers who are interested in using the model in a long-term therapy and with an intensity of two or three sessions per week, should consult *Borderline Personality Disorder and the Conversational Model: A Clinician's Guide* (Meares, 2012a).

The core psychodynamic-interpersonal model therapy

PI therapy is designed for the therapy of clients whose symptoms and problems arise from difficulties or disturbances in interpersonal relationships. It is, therefore, not problem-specific, and it can be used in its basic format to help individuals with a variety of symptomatic complaints. The practical workings of the model can be enhanced by tailoring it to certain conditions (such as depression and medically unexplained symptoms), but the basic underlying process is similar no matter which particular symptom complex the client is experiencing. This is an advantage as clients rarely experience one pure psychiatric disorder. Instead people commonly present with complex multi-symptomatic complaints.

Hobson referred to the process of therapy as 'personal problem solving' (Hobson, 1985). By this he meant the discovery, exploration and solution of significant problems that are brought alive in the therapy. The model assumes that past emotional deprivation, hurts and failures result in difficulties in expressing personal feelings in an appropriate way. Current and past hurt is avoided, resulting in the development of troubling symptoms and behaviours. Hence, PI therapy can be seen within the context of psychodynamic and relational therapies.

PI therapy has at its heart the development of a 'feeling language' between therapist and client. By this we mean a way of talking and exploring emotions with people that 'feels alive' in the conversation and includes symbolic resonances. As discussed in Chapter 1, Hobson differentiates between the kind of language that we use to describe objects (which he refers to as 'jam-jar' language), and the kind of language we use to describe feelings (Hobson, 1985: 19). There is an important difference between a client who talks 'about' things, and a client who talks 'with' the therapist as a person, and shares with him or her 'alive' experiences and feelings, and it is the latter form of communication that the model tries to promote.

The term 'forms of feeling' that Hobson used as the title of his book refers to more than an experience of raw emotion. Hobson referred to complex images, thoughts, processes, memories and experiences that are linked with specific feeling states and personal relating, and ordered in differing levels of coherence. Staying with a feeling, which is one of the central actions of the model (see later), is not just about sharing raw emotion. The intention is to stay with the feeling to see what emerges; what images, memories and complex experiences are linked or connected in some fashion to that particular feeling state. Key problems with interpersonal relating often lie at the heart of these processes, which are captured symbolically by a particular image or memory.

This aim of personal problem-solving occurs through the discovery, exploration and solution of significant problems that are brought alive in the therapeutic conversation. A central feature of the model is the promotion of a symbolic attitude, which is captured by helping clients to *stay with feelings*, and through this to see what emerges. The emphasis is about *how* a conversation is developed, rather than *what* is actually discussed. Key actions of the therapist, described below, were developed by Hobson and his colleagues with the specific intention of generating a *feeling language* from which previously warded off feelings can be faced and assimilated and problems can be identified, explored and resolved. The process involves:

- staying with immediate experiencing;
- working with symbolic language, ideas and images to order and understand experiencing in relation to others;
- owning experiences, and responsibility for actions, and minimising avoidant behaviour; and
- active learning in sessions of different ways of ordering experiences, managing feelings and relating to other.

The process is collaborative and progresses according to the client's needs and wishes, and at a pace that is therapeutic. Hobson used the term *aloneness-togetherness* to capture an ideal form of a collaborative relationship (Hobson, 1985: 194). This is one where there is intimate sharing of feelings and experiences between the therapist and client, yet both retain their individuality and their own inner space. The therapist will disclose little personal information or personal problems, but is an active participant in the relationship with the client, sharing experience and using his/her own intuitive feelings to identify with the client's feeling state. Hobson differentiated aloneness from isolation and loneliness, and togetherness from non-differentiation or fusion.

A great deal can occur between two people within a few minutes, but often important signs or signals or opportunities to explore feelings are missed. Audio or video recording sessions and playing them back enables the therapist to identify and recognise these missed opportunities, and gradually over time to become more receptive to the *minute particulars* of the conversation.

The three competency stages

The competencies are divided into three stages. Stage 1 competencies enable the therapist to establish a close and supportive relationship with the client, and begin to pick up and discuss feelings. Stage 2 competencies encourage the development of a feeling language and a deepening of the therapeutic relationship. Stage 3 competencies are concerned with interpersonal problem-solving once a feeling language has been established.

- Stage 1 competencies are relatively easy to learn and simple to execute. If used collectively, they comprise a powerful tool for establishing a feeling of being understood by the client. They can be used in low-intensity work, without the other model components, to facilitate rapid development of a problem, followed by problem solution. They can be taught to health professionals with no prior knowledge or training in psychotherapy.
- Stage 2 competencies involve a deepening of the relationship and more intense work and can also be learnt quickly by individuals who have good interpersonal skills. However, regular supervision involving recorded sessions from several different clients is required to develop them fully.
- Stage 3 competencies involve the layering and linking together of feelings, ideas, relationships and problems in a cyclical and evolving process. Supervision, using audio recordings, is necessary to develop these skills. Health professionals with a prior training in therapeutic work (e.g. a counselling diploma, or psychodynamic training or CB therapy training) can often learn the components of the model quite quickly, provided they feel a 'natural affinity' with this particular way of working.

Stage 1 competencies

1.1 Statements

The therapist uses statements rather than questions. Questions tend to make the therapeutic situation more one-sided and also tend to push clients into an intellectualised mode as they try to respond or struggle to find an answer. A statement suggests a starting point, and it encourages the client to rest in an experience from which something may emerge. These statements are made in a tentative manner.

Box 4.1   Questions and statements

Using a question

CLIENT: Sometimes my sister just takes over, she's so bossy.

THERAPIST: In what way is she bossy?

CLIENT: Well she tells me how I decorate my house, and she tells me which men I should go out with, and she…

Using a statement

CLIENT: Sometimes my sister just takes over, she's so bossy.

THERAPIST: That sounds difficult.

CLIENT: Yes it is…it makes me feel so frustrated…and…angry.

In the above example the use of a question results in the client giving the therapist more information, whereas the use of a statement results in three important benefits: the client feels understood, it creates an atmosphere of reflection, and from this the client's feelings regarding her sister emerge. Further illustrations of the use of statements are given below:

Box 4.2   Using statements

Example 1

CLIENT: When I got home, I'd barely got through the door, and they [her parents] said they were off to stay the weekend at friends, they just don't seem to care…

THERAPIST: …you felt very let down.

CLIENT: I so wanted to see them,…I felt so hurt.

Example 2

(Early on in the first session, after a long pause)

THERAPIST: It's a bit difficult all this…coming to see someone like me…

CLIENT: Well, yeah, I didn't know what to expect…I don't know what I thought it would be like…it just feels strange.

It is common when people start learning to use the model that they find using statements, rather than asking questions, quite difficult. It is not that questions are forbidden in this model, but rather that statements are generally preferred. There may be times when it is appropriate to use a question if the therapist requires a direct response from the client. Someone who is learning the model should focus on trying to use more statements and fewer questions than they do usually. As they do this, they often begin to see the value in using statements as these help to keep the focus on feelings, and there is a natural shift towards using fewer and fewer specific questions.

1.2 Picking up cues (listening and noticing)

In any model of psychotherapy, it is important that the therapist is vigilant and attentive to what the client is experiencing. This means trying to appreciate, understand and tune into what the client is saying in his/her words, tone of voice and behaviour. In this model, listening is a major part of the work of the therapist. Listening is 'an active process of perceiving and paying attention to a multitude of verbal and non-verbal cues and by an imaginative act, creating possible meanings which can be tried out and modified in a conversation, or dialogue, that aims at understanding' (Hobson, 1985).

Verbal cues

Verbal cues refer to when the client alludes to how he or she is feeling.

Box 4.3   Picking up verbal cues

Example: Fails to pick up a verbal cue

CLIENT: Sometimes I just get so sick and tired of all the hassle.

THERAPIST: What kind of hassle?

CLIENT: Well...it's someone at work...etc.

Example: Picks up cue

CLIENT: Sometimes I just get so sick and tired of all the hassle.

THERAPIST: You sound weary and fed up.

CLIENT: I just can't stand work at present...I wonder if I can carry on...it's just awful!

In the first example above, when the therapist fails to pick up the verbal cue, the client goes on to give an external account of the problem. In the second example, by picking up the verbal cue, the client is encouraged to describe how he/she feels.

Vocal cues

These cues refer to the tonal inflection used by the client when he/she speaks. The client could make a relatively innocuous statement but the tone of his/her voice might, for example, sound angry. There may be more subtle changes in rhythm and intonation that stress particular aspects.

It is not possible to give examples of this kind of cue in written text, but when the therapist responds to it, he/she should acknowledge the evidence on which it is based. Instead of just saying, 'you're angry' the therapist should say '...what you said just now – there was a real sting in your voice, I wonder if you sometimes feel quite angry inside'. This will make more sense to the client and will also make the client feel that the therapist is listening to him/her and trying to understand.

Non-verbal cues

Non-verbal cues include all other kinds of behaviour that the client may exhibit during the therapy. They include the client's facial expression and demeanour, eye contact, body language, clothing, personal items and behaviour outside the therapy room. They can be fairly straightforward, for example the client look-ing sad, or they can be much more complex, for example the client avoiding eye contact whenever referring to himself or the therapist.

When the therapist comments on a non-verbal cue, it is important to gauge how receptive the client is to such an observation. For some clients it can feel very intrusive, for others it can be an enormous relief. Observations should be couched in a tentative manner, particularly if the cue is rather complex and subtle and also if the cue refers to the client–therapist relationship. If the client appears receptive, then the therapist can go on to suggest possible feel-ings that may underlie the client's actions, but expressed in a tentative way. Or, the client may spontaneously develop the theme.

Box 4.4 Responses to non-verbal cues

THERAPIST: You look really sad today.

THERAPIST: I can see that you're screwing up your fists...you seem...very angry.

THERAPIST: When I confirmed just now we'll be finishing meeting in six weeks' time, you looked...umh...you looked to me quite stunned...[pause to see if client accepts this]...as if it was a surprise...

> THERAPIST: I'm not sure, but when you said you were going to miss me during the break…you turned your head away and looked down…as if…well…you didn't want to or couldn't look at me…[pause to see if this is denied or accepted and to see if client responds]…
>
> THERAPIST: This may be quite difficult for you, but I've been aware that since we've been meeting for these last four weeks, you've never really been able to look at me…you know…look me in the eye…[pause again to see whether client can tolerate this observation]…

Cues in the therapist

The ways that the therapist behaves or feels can, on some occasions, provide clues as to how the client is feeling in the therapy session. This idea is based upon the psychodynamic theories of counter transference. These theories suggest that the therapist can sometimes act as either a resonating board and pick up the same feeling as the client is actually feeling in the session, or act as a depository so that the therapist experiences a feeling but the client has no sense of experiencing it.

This is a highly complex area and supervision is important in disentangling the different elements – even for very experienced therapists. The therapist has to be able to distinguish his/her own personal feelings from feelings that are more closely related to the client. This is difficult as there is usually a great deal of overlap between the two, and the client's feelings may well resonate with some of the therapist's own emotionally vulnerable areas.

For example, the therapist may begin to feel irritated with the client for no obvious reason. This may not be related directly to the therapy and could be related to the therapist's own personal issues which have intruded into the session. It is important, however, that the therapist reflects upon the unusual feeling and asks himself/herself whether it could be intimating something important about the interpersonal situation with the client too. It is possible that, in this example, the therapist may be picking up that the client is actually very angry with him/her, but, is not expressing this directly. The therapist is picking up the theme of anger, although this was initially experienced as related to personal issues, but it may have several sources that are not mutually exclusive.

1.3 Negotiation

The 'how' of the therapist's talk is crucial: the therapist should not imply that he or she is right. The therapist is really trying to say to the client, 'This is how I see things now, but I might not be right; I may have misunderstood; I'd like you to help me see things clearer'. This attitude produces an atmosphere of collaboration between the client and therapist where deeper understanding is reached through a series of gradual adjustments of meaning which get closer and closer to the client's experience. It is also a way of pacing the therapy so that the client does not feel either overwhelmed, or intruded upon, by the therapist.

The client should feel able to reject any suggestion from the therapist, even if the therapist thinks that he/she is right. In some circumstances, the therapist's statement may be accurate but unacceptable to the client in the form in which it has been presented. Accuracy is not always therapeutic.

Box 4.5   Illustrating negotiation

Example 1: Non-negotiating

CLIENT: I think if people are in professional jobs they should be trustworthy, if they say they're going to turn up [talking about a nurse not turning up for a home visit], they should!

THERAPIST: I think that you feel angry because I was late today.

CLIENT: You what?…no I'm not angry with you.

Example 2: Negotiating

CLIENT: I think if people are in professional jobs they should be trustworthy, if they say they're going to turn up [talking about nurse not turning up for a home visit], they should!

THERAPIST: You seem very upset about this…I wonder if your upset is also partly about something similar to what you describe…in that I turned up quite late today…I'm not sure.

CLIENT: I was annoyed with you.

THERAPIST: I thought that you were, but I wasn't sure…it's quite a big thing for you.

CLIENT: Yes, when I was little my mother was always, always late…I cannot stand it, I really cannot stand it.

In the first example above, the therapist's statement is too direct. The client cannot deal with it and blocks. In the second example the therapist first of all acknowledges the client's distress and then tentatively suggests a possible link. The statement is phrased in such a way that the client could easily reject the suggestion if it still seemed too intrusive. The use of phrases like 'I'm not sure', 'I wonder', 'This may not be quite right', etc. invite the client to subtly provide corrections and refinements to the important details that are being discussed.

The first example could be salvaged if the therapist was able to acknowledge that he/she had made a mistake.

Box 4.6 Acknowledging mistakes

CLIENT: I think if people in professional jobs should be trustworthy, if they say they're going to turn up [talking about nurse not turning up for a home visit], they should!

THERAPIST: You feel angry because I was late today.

CLIENT: You what?...no I'm not angry with you.

THERAPIST: I've not got that right...it seemed as if it was a very important thing for you, people not turning up or letting you down...

CLIENT: It is...

THERAPIST: ...Something really gets to you inside.

CLIENT: Yes, when I was little my mum always, always turned up late...it was a family joke...but...I can't bear it.

THERAPIST: I thought it was really important for you...which is why I wondered whether me being late this morning had an effect on you.

CLIENT: Well I was slightly annoyed by it...but I know you're very busy... it's not like with my mother...she's got all the time in the world.

THERAPIST: Well, let's see, there's something similar between how you felt this morning about me when I was late and how you feel about your mum,...but also something that makes that feeling feel different.

By initially retracting the first statement, the therapist has now enabled the client to explore the link between her anger towards the therapist and her own mother. The client can go on to explore with the therapist her view that the therapist is very busy and therefore cannot be blamed for being late. This will be a rich and complex area for discovery and mutual understanding.

Negotiating is particularly helpful when it is used to explore issues involving the relationship between the client and the therapist. The following example illustrates this. It is quite long as it attempts to convey the process of negotiation.

Box 4.7 The process of negotiation

CLIENT: You're bound to be judging me, no matter what you say, you can't sit there and not have an opinion.

THERAPIST: ...Umh...well...I do have some impressions of you, but...you said judging you...it implies possibly that you may think...or fear that I'm...judging you in a bad light?...

(Continued)

(Continued)

CLIENT: ...yeah...

THERAPIST: umh...criticising.

CLIENT: Yeah,...I think you must be sitting there thinking how dull and boring I am.

THERAPIST: I'd like to understand this a bit more...it sounds...very painful.

CLIENT: Yeah, it's really hard...

THERAPIST: You feel on edge with me,...not comfortable...at all.

CLIENT: I just feel you must think I'm pathetic.

THERAPIST   ...umh.........weak?

CLIENT: Yeah, weak and pathetic and useless...

THERAPIST: Well, you want to know what I think of you...yet you fear what I think of you...you feel criticised... you feel this weakness inside...it feels sort of exposing?...

CLIENT: Yeah...

THERAPIST: Yes...and...I...wonder...this situation now...you and me...makes you feel a bit cross?

CLIENT: Cross with myself...angry with myself for being so pathetic...

THERAPIST: Well... [hesitantly]

CLIENT: I know I don't have to be here...no one's forcing me to come here and see you, but I couldn't not just turn up...I should be able to...just not let it bother me...just tell people to get lost.

THERAPIST: ...and here, with me, suppose you felt you wanted to say...'why don't you shut up and stop asking these questions...stop looking at me...I'm not putting myself through this any more'...

CLIENT: No...no...[smiling]...no I couldn't do that.

THERAPIST: Well perhaps could we look at that...I wonder what the feeling would be...

1.4 Understanding hypotheses

Hypotheses in the PI therapy are ways of promoting exploration and understanding of the client's feelings, especially in interpersonal relationships. There are some similarities between hypotheses and interpretations – which are also exploratory statements – as used in other kinds of interpersonal and dynamic therapies. Hypotheses, however, are offered with much less certainty and conviction than interpretations commonly are, and they are usually couched in more subtle language than interpretations, which are usually more direct and unambiguous.

The aim of a hypothesis is to engage the client in a dialogue concerning its accuracy. It is always better expressed in a tentative manner so it can be accepted, rejected or modified by the client. Of importance is the communication of a desire to understand, not necessarily to get it right.

These are statements made by the therapist that refer to how he/she imagines the client is feeling. They are usually based upon subtle non-verbal cues or are responses to verbal cues from the client. They are not mere reflections of the client's feelings but an attempt on the part of the therapist to take the exploration of the client's feelings a little further.

Box 4.8   Understanding hypotheses

Example 1

CLIENT: I'm edgy, I can't settle…

THERAPIST: I'd like to hear a bit more about that…seems you feel sort of wound-up.

Example 2

CLIENT: I feel dead inside.

THERAPIST: …it's hard to feel anything at all…empty…

Example 3

THERAPIST: I wonder if you're feeling a bit stuck right now.

Although the use of filling words like 'sort of' or 'a bit' may appear rather unnecessary in the examples above, they reduce the harshness and starkness of the statements, making them more acceptable for the client.

Summary

The four Stage 1 competencies of PI therapy have been described above. They are: using statements; picking up cues; negotiating style; and understanding hypotheses. They are relatively easy to learn and can be picked up quickly by health professionals who have good interpersonal skills, and they can be used together in a coherent form (Guthrie et al., 2004b). Cue response is an area that can always be improved, as even the most experienced therapists miss or fail to recognise important cues.

These basic skills lay the foundation for the development of a strong working relationship with a client. They encourage people to share how they are feeling with the therapist, rather than talk about problems in a detached or abstract way. They promote a feeling of being listened to and understood. The next chapter will describe the four Stage 2 competencies.

5

Intermediate Psychodynamic-Interpersonal Skills

Introduction

This chapter describes the second stage competencies of PI therapy. They are slightly more challenging to learn than the Stage 1 competencies but their use leads to a deepening of the relationship between therapist and client. When used collectively, they promote the development of a *feeling language* and sharing of experience.

Stage 2 competencies

2.1 Focusing on feelings ('here and now')

This technique involves focusing on what the client is experiencing during the session. Instead of talking about feelings in the abstract or as if they belong only to the past, an attempt is made to re-create them or facilitate the actual expression of them in the immediacy of the therapeutic environment. The client experiences the feeling and is able to share it with the therapist.

Box 5.1   Here and now

Example 1: Not using 'here' and 'now'

CLIENT: When my grandmother died, I didn't say goodnight to her before she went to bed, when I woke up the next morning, my mum came in and told me she had died in the night...I know it seems a small thing...I know she knew that I loved her...but it really used to upset me...that I hadn't said goodnight...and...that was the last time I saw her.

THERAPIST: You must have been very upset.

CLIENT: Yes I was, it seems such a long time ago though.

Example 2: Using the 'here and now'

CLIENT: When my grandmother died, I didn't say goodnight to her before she went to bed, when I woke up the next morning, my mum came in and told me she had died in the night..I know it seems a small thing...I know she knew that I loved her...but it really used to upset me...that I hadn't said goodnight...and...that was the last time I saw her.

THERAPIST: And there's something of that upset and sadness now...you feel it now...here...with me.

CLIENT: Uh yes...

THERAPIST: Can we stay with that feeling.

CLIENT: [cries]

In the first example above, although the therapist acknowledges that the client must have been very distressed, because the therapist uses the past tense the actual feelings remain in the past and inaccessible. In the second example, because the therapist focuses upon the present, the client is able to get in touch with these feelings that previously have been buried.

This technique should only be used if the therapist senses that the client is actually experiencing the feeling, even if it is only mild, although he/she finds it difficult to acknowledge directly. If the client appears completely detached and unemotional, such a response from the therapist would be inappropriate. In these circumstances, it would be better for the therapist to contrast the distress described by the client, with the *lack* of feeling he/she is actually experiencing, although this needs tact as the client may not yet be aware of the discrepancy.

Another way of helping people get in touch with feelings is to ask them to relive experiences as if they were happening 'now'. The therapist asks the client to use the present tense to describe something from the past, as if it were happening 'now'. The event has already been identified as a significant one that the client has remembered as having some specific meaning or importance for them.

Box 5.2 Here and now (continued)

THERAPIST: I suppose...could you tell me...just let it come to mind...any time when you were small...we when you were really wanting your mum to be close to you.

CLIENT: Er...

THERAPIST: And were upset about it.

CLIENT: Er...I was eight. My mother had another child. When I came home, she went into hospital. I knew she was going into hospital to have a baby. That night she did go in. I can still remember it...five or seven days...I'm not sure how long it was. It was when she did come home – when she did come home, my mother was angry...and from that point onwards I don't think she treated me any different...because I was always as my mother would say a sickly child, I would get a lot of things, my other sisters felt sorry for me, but I didn't know this at the time. I'm not sure if I felt jealousy for my youngest sister. I was eight then...

THERAPIST: But your mother was angry.

CLIENT: Yes I don't know why...because she was always very kind. It took a lot to get her angry. And I did walk in and she did have a lot of visitors there that day, and I don't know if I said anything but she appeared to be very angry and that affected me for some reason and I've never forgotten that.

THERAPIST: Yes...I wonder if we could go through that bit, almost as if it's happening now. Conjure up a picture.

CLIENT: Yes I can still picture it.

THERAPIST: Right well now can you talk about it as if it's happening now.

CLIENT: Right.

THERAPIST: Where are you? Can you say 'I am' not 'I was'?

CLIENT: Well there were a few people.

THERAPIST: I am [indicates with hand]...There are...

CLIENT: Oh...I am...I walked into the room...

THERAPIST: You are walking...

CLIENT: I'm walking to the door...my mother and a few other ladies were speaking...

THERAPIST: are...[gestures with hand]...there they are...

CLIENT: I'd say I'm in...In the lounge by this stage...and I must have said something to my mother...I'm not sure...

(Continued)

(Continued)

THERAPIST: You see how hard you are finding it…to say as if it's happening now… it isn't easy…to say it as if it's happening now…I must have said something…I don't know what it is…but my mom…

CLIENT: She snapped.

THERAPIST: Snapped…as if she's doing it now.

CLIENT: Yes…she snapped at me and that affected me…maybe because she'd never snapped at me before the baby was born…so therefore I took it very hard…that's the only way I can describe that.

THERAPIST: Well when you say you took it very hard…let's imagine what that feeling was like.

CLIENT: A hurt feeling.

THERAPIST: Feels like I'm really hurt.

CLIENT: Very hurt…very hurt.

THERAPIST: Deep down inside.

CLIENT: Very hurt and I thought, she wasn't like that before she had the baby.

THERAPIST: Well…stay with it now…stay with the feeling.

CLIENT: Yes very hurt…I feel that…… just comes over me…from here [points to tummy] upwards. [Points to head]

[Therapist mirrors action]

CLIENT: This horrible hurt feeling, why did she snap at me?

THERAPIST: Aaaand…maybe she doesn't love me anymore.

CLIENT: Right… [long pause]…yes I suppose that is the feeling.

In the example in Box 5.2 the therapist and client explore an important memory from the client's childhood. The therapist encourages the client to try to re-experience the memory, as if it is happening 'now'. This approach is only used for memories that are likely to have significant emotional meaning, and where the client finds it difficult to get back in touch with feelings.

Note how, in the first part of the example, the client is gradually remembering some facts about what happened, but seems hazy about what was experienced. The client knows something important happened between her and her mother that has stuck with her. The therapist pushes quite hard to help the client relive the associated feelings.

There are two main reasons for trying to focus on feelings within the PI model. First, some feelings may be difficult to acknowledge and share. For example, someone who feels angry following the death of a loved one, may not be able to acknowledge this feeling, as it may seem unacceptable. Other feelings may be warded off because they are too frightening to acknowledge or embarrassing. Beginning to experience a warded off feeling in the presence of a supportive other can be therapeutic and cathartic, and lead to change (Box 5.3).

Box 5.3 Getting in touch with a warded off feeling

A young mother developed feelings of intense anxiety about her baby daughter and was unable to leave her in the company of others (even her own mother) without developing panic attacks. Brief cognitive behavioural treatment had not been successful as she was too anxious to carry out the homework or tolerate any separation from her baby.

Initially in the sessions, which she attended with her baby, she described herself as having anxiety all the time. This started around the time her baby was born. She said the birth had been difficult but she had got over it, and didn't think it was connected to her current problem. The therapist noticed that she used the word 'anxiety' to describe how she felt and never elaborated upon this: 'It's my anxiety, it just stops me from doing anything.'

THERAPIST: Your anxiety...I'd like to try and understand more...get a feeling of what it feels like for you...what you actually experience...

CLIENT: Anxiety...it's my anxiety.

THERAPIST: A feeling inside?

CLIENT: Anxiety. [Client responds several times to gentle probes by the therapist, each time responding with the word 'anxiety'.]

THERAPIST: A feeling in your body...perhaps...a tenseness?

CLIENT: Yes...a shakiness...[Makes a fluttering gesture with her hands.]

THERAPIST: It's there a bit now?...this shakiness [makes similar fluttering gesture]

CLIENT: Yes...[client noticeably becomes more anxious]

THERAPIST: ...with the tenseness and the shakiness...there's a fear...

CLIENT: Yes...[breathing more heavily]...that she's going to die...Hayley's going to die...

THERAPIST: Like it's really going to happen...or you thought she had?

CLIENT: Like when she were born, I was out of it, it was forceps and she was taken to the special care unit. But I didn't know, so when I woke up, she weren't there, she weren't there...and I thought she died...and I just began wailing...until one of the midwives came in...but I couldn't

(Continued)

> *(Continued)*
>
> stop shaking until they took me up to the unit to see her...it's like I didn't believe them...
>
> THERAPIST: You thought she'd died.
>
> CLIENT: Yes...it were terrible...terrible. We'd been trying for ages...I'd kept miscarrying and I thought...all through the pregnancy...I thought I was going to lose her. Like all the other babies...I just knew it.
>
> THERAPIST: You've had a really terrible time...so many lost babies...it's really difficult to cope with all that loss.
>
> CLIENT: I blame myself...[Client is connected and talking closely with the therapist.]

In this example, the therapist is able to help the client get in touch with feelings that lie behind her 'anxiety'; the terrible fear that her baby had died and that in some way she may be responsible for this.

The second reason for focusing on feelings in this model is to encourage the connection between feelings and symbolic thought processes. The feelings have to be present and experienced by the client for this process to happen, otherwise it becomes an intellectual exercise. The notion of 'forms of feelings' has already been discussed in the first chapter in this book and in the introduction to the manual (Chapter 4). It implies a complex system of connected feelings and images, which arise from and are woven into the fabric of interpersonal relating. As the person experiences and stays in touch with a feeling, certain thoughts, images or ideas 'come into mind'.

2.2 Metaphor and living symbols

Use of metaphor in literature refers to the fusing of two or more images and/or ideas to bring a new experience and a new order and meaning. Metaphor is not exclusive to PI therapy, but it is used commonly by PI therapists to bring vividness to an idea, to expand understanding of an experience or concept, and to deepen the level of emotional exchange between the client and the therapist. The therapist should be alert to the language that the client uses to describe his/her experience.

It is often by 'staying with' immediate experience (focus on feelings) that nascent images, symbols and ideas emerge. In this model, the emphasis is not on what a symbol might mean, or why a particular metaphor has been used. The interest is in where they might lead the conversation. The therapist aims to convey and promote a *symbolical attitude*.

This means endowing words, gestures, experiences, and dreams with value; regarding them not only as communications of formulated messages but also as living symbols. They are intimations of, and means of apprehending, what is as yet unknown. (Hobson, 1985: 199)

Box 5.4   Using metaphors

Example 1

CLIENT: I feel on edge all the time…I just can't settle.

THERAPIST: Sounds as if you feel…sort of wound up.

CLIENT: I feel myself getting tighter and tighter inside…everything's rigid…

THERAPIST: Feels a bit like you feel like a spring…that's all coiled up…being turned tighter and tighter.

CLIENT: Yeah, I think sometimes people do things deliberately to wind me up…I'm sure I'm going to just snap.

Example 2

CLIENT: I feel trapped…there's no way out…nothing to look forward to…nothing's going to change.

THERAPIST: It all feels quite hopeless…

CLIENT: Yeah.

THERAPIST: …as if you can't move…stuck.

CLIENT: I can't…I can't do anything.

THERAPIST: It's a bit like…you feel like almost caught in some kind of trap…like perhaps an animal caught in a trap.

CLIENT: I always feel sorry for animals…like that…I hate hunting…it's so cruel…it's so unfair, the animal hasn't done anything wrong…it's an awful death…so painful and frightening…

THERAPIST: Hmm.

CLIENT: It's so unfair…what have I done to deserve this.

In both of the examples in Box 5.4, the therapist picks up and extends the metaphor initially voiced by the client. There is a movement, a carrying forward. In the first example, the extension of the metaphor leads to a deepening of the feeling language, and to a new insight. That is, that the experience of being 'on edge' is linked to an interpersonal dynamic (a feeling that people are deliberately trying to upset the client).

In the second example, the feeling of being trapped is elaborated, and there is movement from 'stuckness' to the client's 'here and now' experience of being an 'innocent creature' who is hunted and persecuted. Note at the beginning the therapist is active in developing the metaphor, but later leaves space with just a small encouragement for the client to stay with the exploration.

In *Forms of Feeling*, Bob Hobson describes seeing a client called 'Joe Smith' (Hobson, 1985: 33). Joe finds it difficult to describe how he feels and to put his feelings into words. Hobson encourages him to stay with the difficulty of being in touch with himself and Joe blurts out that there isn't anything inside, there is 'no me'. After a longish pause, Joe says, 'I feel queer'. Hobson asks Joe to stay with the feeling, but Joe becomes very tense and begins to feel scared. He loses touch with the feeling and then noticeably relaxes. Something, however, has been shared. A few weeks later the feeling emerges again and this time he is able to stay with it. Joe describes a 'wobbly feeling' and from this, he and the therapist get to a feeling of 'being wobbly like a child trying to walk'. A symbolic transformation has occurred. The original experience of 'feeling queer' has been transformed into a shared personal feeling between the therapist and client, involving fears about being little and vulnerable, and fears about 'leaving mum'. This process only occurred because the therapist adopted an attitude of expectant waiting, what Hobson called a 'symbolic attitude' and encouraged Joe to stay with the feeling of 'queer' (see Chapter 6 for further discussion of a 'symbolic attitude').

This example demonstrates that an important metaphor can hold together an important theme across sessions. When looking in more detail at assimilation in psychotherapy we found that this ongoing shared reference to a key idea was highly characteristic of PI therapy and often the theme could be brought back in a subsequent session just by either the client or the therapist mentioning the key phrase as a shared reference point (Stiles et al., 1990).

2.3 Language of mutuality ('I and we')

The therapist explicitly refers to the relationship between therapist and client in terms of first-person words 'I' and 'we'. This indicates an active and mutual involvement in exploration. It also facilitates a deepening of the relationship between the therapist and the client, and accentuates a directness of communication. Some examples are given in Box 5.5.

Box 5.5   Examples of using a language of mutuality

- I'd like you to stay with that feeling if you can?
- I can imagine how difficult that was for you.
- I think that you're feeling that a bit now, that feeling of upset…here with me.
- I'd like to try and get a better understanding of how you are feeling.
- Maybe it's something that you and I can work together on?

This component of the model sounds simple and straightforward but it can have a surprisingly powerful effect when used, and usually results in a deepening of the conversation and a focus on what is happening between the client and the therapist at that moment in therapy (see Box 5.6).

Box 5.6   Example of deepening the conversation using 'I and we'

Not using 'I' and 'we'

THERAPIST: It seems like an effort to come here.

Using 'I' and 'we'

THERAPIST: I wonder if you feel it's an effort to come here and see me.

The shift in language is subtle, but the accumulated effect is significant as it models personal language and avoids abstractions like 'It's'. The example also shows the therapist being tentative at the same time, which is easier to achieve when using personal language. It also focuses the therapy on the relationship between the therapist and client, and on the 'problem', which is alive in the session between the two people.

If the therapist starts to use passive or abstract language when referring to the client–therapist relationship, it may be a sign in this model that the therapist and client are not connected. It can even imply on occasions that the therapist is avoiding uncomfortable or difficult feelings that he/she feels the client holds towards him or her.

2.4 Linking hypotheses

Linking hypotheses are statements that link feelings that have emerged in the therapy sessions to other feelings both inside and outside the therapy. They are a way of drawing links between the client–therapist relationship and other important relationships in the client's life, past or present. In this respect, they may refer to the transference relationship between the client and therapist, although this is not always the case.

Box 5.7   Examples of linking hypotheses

THERAPIST: Maybe some of the feelings you've had here of worrying whether I would take you seriously are a bit like feelings you've had at work worrying whether people would believe you.

THERAPIST :   I wonder if the way you feel now...a bit unsure of me...a bit worried whether you can trust me...is a bit like...a little bit like...like you were saying earlier...finding it difficult to trust your dad because you didn't know whether he'd hug you or beat you...

These examples show the link being made between the relationship between therapist and client, to other relationships. The first example is to a current outside relationship at work, and the second to a past experience with a relationship with the client's father. At this point the therapist is simply establishing the link but not drawing any general conclusions from it. That step could occur later once the link has been established.

Linking hypotheses are used by the therapist to create a pattern of interlinking relationships or themes, which gradually build as the therapy progresses. The links can be vertical (i.e. referring to past or childhood relationships) or horizontal (referring to current relationships outside therapy) or both. A more coherent picture begins to emerge as the links that are made resonate with the present and the current difficulties or problems facing the client.

Summary

The four Stage 2 competencies that have been described in this chapter are powerful therapeutic tools, and care and experience are required to use them appropriately and wisely. They enable the therapy to 'come alive' and for experiences to be shared rather than talked about. In the next chapter, the Stage 3 competencies will be described that deal with the ways in which the session can be used to help the client to structure their experiences into a coherent shape and then begin to address their difficulties.

6

Advanced Psychodynamic-Interpersonal Skills

Introduction

This chapter describes the remaining five key competencies of PI therapy: explanatory hypotheses, PI therapy rationale, sequencing of intervention, relating interpersonal change to therapy and patterns in relationships. These help the therapist to explore the client's problem in depth and facilitate the development of a coherent and shared description of the problem. At the end of this chapter we also discuss problematic behaviours that the therapist should avoid. These are rarely discussed in therapy manuals, but we believe a fundamental aspect of any therapeutic endeavour is not to do harm and we include some guidance on what to avoid.

Stage 3 competencies

3.1 Explanatory hypotheses

These statements are more complex than understanding or linking hypotheses (see Chapters 4 and 5) and are only made after the therapist has acquired considerable information about the client. There will have been preparatory work with understanding and linking hypotheses before extending to an explanatory hypothesis. This type of hypothesis introduces the possibility of underlying reasons for problems and difficulties in relationships. They usually relate to a repeated pattern of maladaptive behaviour, both inside and outside of therapy, and have often been present in the past – often detectable in some form even as far back as childhood – as well as the present. The therapist tries to link the client's behaviour to some kind of underlying conflict or difficulty. This provides an opportunity for the conflict to be acknowledged, owned and explored. It may also lead to other ways of dealing with the underlying difficulty as the seemingly blocked patterns become available for reflective thinking.

Box 6.1   Example of an explanatory hypothesis

THERAPIST: You were saying that it's hard for you to feel angry with me...even though it seems justified and appropriate, and...that I kept you waiting this morning. You've also said that you find it difficult to feel angry with other people even when they mistreat you. Your dad, of course, was a very angry and violent man...I wonder if you're afraid somehow that if you were to get annoyed with me, you might lose control and get very angry...or maybe that I would get very angry...a bit like your dad used to...and either way...that's very scary.

In the above example, before giving the explanation, the therapist provided three pieces of information on which the hypothesis was based. This is important, as otherwise it may sound as if the therapist is conjuring the hypothesis out of thin air. The pieces of information, however, need not necessarily be given in the one statement and may emerge in the context of a dialogue between the client and therapist over several minutes. The client may well contribute to the links too, and help to prepare the ground for the therapist to pick out the pattern for further exploration. This example shows how an exploratory hypothesis may be embedded within a conversation.

Box 6.2   Explanatory hypothesis in conversation

CLIENT: I feel as if I've always got to fit in...please others...I end up with no say over my life...I don't ever say what I want.

THERAPIST: You kind of adapt yourself to others.

CLIENT: Yeah I end up not knowing what I want, whether it's something I really want or something that she wants, or something my mother wants, or something I'm expected to want.

THERAPIST: It's all mixed up...your feelings...

CLIENT: Yeah.

THERAPIST: It seems one of the scary things about getting close...is you're not sure who is you and who is the other person...Sheila...your mother...

CLIENT: Yeah...

THERAPIST:	...and...if you don't fit in...please others...you could be hurt?
CLIENT:	I don't know if I let myself be hurt...I cut off...I say I don't care.
THERAPIST:	Umh...
CLIENT:	I don't know what to do...with...with feeling this...this hurt.
THERAPIST:	It's scary...scary staying with it a little while...with me.
CLIENT:	Umh...
THERAPIST:	It seems...you want to be close...but you're scared of being close... 'cause you feel taken over...or you can't tell, who is who, kind of...so you cut yourself off...but then you feel awful inside...lonely?
CLIENT:	People think I'm so easy going...so nice...yet they don't see how alone I feel.
THERAPIST:	Alone because it's so scary to be close.

In the above example, the client and therapist eventually reach an understanding of why the client is scared of relationships, and why he keeps himself at a distance.

3.2 PI therapy rationale

An essential component of PI therapy is an understanding between the client and therapist of the purpose of therapy. This may evolve during the first session as the client's experiences and problems are shared and explored. A strong rationale for focusing on feelings and relationships should arise naturally from the shared experiences and discussions between the client and therapist. Towards the end of the first session, or earlier if appropriate, the therapist should make a connection between the importance of focusing upon relationships and sharing experiences in the 'here and now' as a way of facing warded off fears and overcoming problems. This shared rationale can help to build and maintain the therapeutic alliance and provides the client with the beginnings of a model, to understand his/her problems, which can grow and develop as therapy progresses.

Box 6.3   Example of an exploratory therapy rationale

THERAPIST:	Before we finish...can you just say something about your dad...we've not mentioned him.
CLIENT:	Well as a child he would give us a lot of things...but he would also get very angry...at times, which would scare me a lot...and once when I was 13...he came into the room...and was very angry...but he didn't

(Continued)

(Continued)

> hit me...he looked at me...and I was so white, I was that scared that I froze...but I didn't realise I had gone white and he just looked at me, and it shocked him that I had got so scared, and he walked out...and later on when he told someone about it...... shocked me that I had got so scared...that's all I can say about my father.

THERAPIST: This anger and violence comes in again.

CLIENT: Yes, but he was very loving...But, he would hit us...that's all I can say.

THERAPIST: You've been able to share that with me.

CLIENT: Yes I have...I've never spoken about what we've talked about just then...and I'm thinking about that now.

THERAPIST: Now we're going to end. Things that are frightening...Often, if you can look them straight in the face...they can often be a lot better...I'd like to end by you telling me again about the dream with the dead people.

CLIENT: Yes well there's two kinds of dreams, one that I had to walk through a road...a narrow road, and all dead people were lying everywhere and behind that was a cemetery, and I was closing my eyes on either side because I didn't want to see the dead people, they were covered, I couldn't see their faces...and there was another time when I had to walk into a room...and all dead people again, bodies...just lying there...and I wake up very disturbed but I don't understand why...why always death?

THERAPIST: You're very scared of death?

CLIENT: Yes.

THERAPIST: We've shared that a bit here.

CLIENT: Yes.

THERAPIST: I think there are important things to explore here...and it's more important to get in touch with that feeling...which I think you were a bit just now...of loss...of fear...than any long explanations.

This extended example shows how encouragement to explore, giving a therapeutic rationale, and some preliminary attempts to link experiences, are all arising within a conversation. The most important aspect of the work is to gain the client's trust and to enable the client to share something of what he or she is feeling in the session. This does not have to involve an elaborate explanation or formulation of the client's problems. A simple, shared understanding that there are difficult or upsetting things in the client's life that may be helpful to share and explore, is usually sufficient for a preliminary rationale. The key is that the feelings, as in the above example ('you are very scared of death') are actually experienced in the session, rather than discussed in an intellectual or theoretical way. The therapist does not say, 'you have a fear of death' the therapist says, 'you are very scared of death'. This difference is subtle but crucial in developing a therapeutic rationale as the former conveys an idea, whilst the latter conveys a lived, current experience.

3.3 Sequencing of intervention

Psychotherapy is a creative process of personal problem-solving. Problems are manifest and explored in the therapeutic conversation. This process begins with the bringing of experiences and feelings into the 'here and now'. Avoidance actions are abandoned and a degree of conflict and stress is tolerated. The connection between feelings and key relationships becomes apparent and possible solutions are created through an imaginative feeling-language.

In PI therapy the sequence always begins with the client's experiences and feelings as they are experienced in the 'here and now'. Sequencing may happen over a few moments where there is clear movement from 'here and now' feelings to their connection to an interpersonal relationship to the possibility of problem solution. However, the process can progress over a whole session or several sessions. The key to this competency is that the therapist is not looking for an immediate explanation for the client's symptoms, so statements like, 'I wonder why you feel like this?' would be out of model behaviours as they are encouraging the client to think 'about' the problem and its cause, rather than get in touch with the problem, and begin to face warded off or difficult feelings.

In the previous example of Joe Smith (see the section on metaphor in Chapter 5) there is a clear sequencing of events. An experience of feeling 'queer' is brought alive in the session. This is felt to be scary and the client moves away from it, but its significance is noted and the shared feeling between client and therapist has signalled a movement in the therapy. Some weeks later the feeling re-emerges and again, by staying with the feeling, Joe describes feeling wobbly in his middle. Hobson links this feeling to the experience of feeling 'wobbly like a child trying to walk' and from this to the feelings of a small child in relation to his mother, which can then be experienced and explored. The warded-off experience that Joe found so threatening has been shared and the possibilities of facing his fears of vulnerability and insecurity have begun. All this has happened in the context of the relationship with the therapist.

3.4 Relating interpersonal change to therapy

In PI therapy the problems are directly presented in the relationship with the therapist as well as being enacted in the client's personal life. Sharing of experiences between the therapist and client and sharing a 'new language' open up fresh avenues of perceiving and acting in the world. As therapy progresses these changes can be acknowledged and understood in a reciprocal and cyclical fashion. Such a process strengthens change and motivation in the client.

Box 6.4 Example of relating interpersonal change to therapy

THERAPIST: So…instead of giving in…in your usual fashion…you actually said no?

CLIENT: Yes, I know…I can't believe it…and when I said it…I thought he'd be really angry [husband] and I got really panicky and for a moment I nearly said…ok…let's go and see her [husband's mother]…but I just didn't say anything…

THERAPIST: It must have been very hard.

CLIENT: Yes…I thought my chest was actually going to burst…my head was pounding…and I was just waiting for him to explode…but he didn't… and eventually I said…that I felt I needed a bit of time at the weekend to sort out the things I need to sort out…and I wasn't saying I would never see his mother…just that…it was too much…and I ended up with no time…to do all the other things…and he could go by himself…

THERAPIST: This is a big…big step for you.

CLIENT: Yes.

THERAPIST: A big change…facing something you thought would result in Bill being very angry…

CLIENT: Yes…but I think he knows…I've changed a bit…since coming to see you…I think he's aware I'm a little different…you know I almost think…he's a bit scared now of shouting at me…because…I'm not as frightened anymore.

THERAPIST: Facing some of those fears with me…has helped?

CLIENT: Yes…yes most definitely.

The client is ready to acknowledge that new patterns are beginning to emerge, and can see that the sessions are assisting that process.

3.5 Patterns in relationships

As the relationship deepens between the therapist and client and more of the client's life is known, repeated patterns in relationships often become apparent. The therapist can use linking hypotheses to help foster the recognition of similarities between relationships. Linking hypotheses may lead on to the recognition of actual maladaptive patterns that occur in two or more of the client's relationships.

Box 6.5   Example of patterns in relationships

CLIENT:	I don't know where to start...
THERAPIST:	There's something difficult perhaps you want to say to me?
CLIENT:	I suddenly realised when I walked out of this room last time that you look like Helen. [Ex-girlfriend with whom client is still obsessed]
THERAPIST:	That is curious.
CLIENT:	F***ing curious!
THERAPIST:	Also curious that it struck you just at the point you were leaving me last week.
CLIENT:	It's been bugging me. I've been sitting down stairs in a real panic as to whether you would turn up. It seemed a bit later this morning...I was in a real panic...then I remembered I saw your light...another thing...I realised I behaved towards Helen exactly the same way I've behaved towards Dawn.
THERAPIST:	You've seen a link between your relationship with Helen...and Dawn...and I'm in there as well on some level.
CLIENT:	When I got on the train, I made a list of my old girlfriends...all had bad problems with relationships with blokes...all depressive...I knew they were damaged from the word go. I want to know what's that about.
THERAPIST:	You've seen a pattern in the type of women you are attracted to... they have problems...there's depression...there's a sense you know they are vulnerable...it's not going to work...
CLIENT:	Yes I just go round and round...
THERAPIST:	Well...I wonder if we could go back to how you felt this morning... before you saw me...there's something of a connection between me and Helen...you said you felt 'panicky'...a fear I wouldn't be there?

An important set of links has been made, with associated powerful feelings in the client. The example ends with the therapist putting down a marker that this has been important and suggesting that they go back and explore the links more deeply.

Developing the conversation

The 13 competencies described in the last three chapters should be used seamlessly and interchangeably in developing a therapeutic conversation. The intention is to move towards a 'mutual dialogue and understanding' with the client. Psychotherapy involves, however, a special kind of conversation in which the two participants have an asymmetrical relationship.

The therapist does not talk about the same things as the client, nor does the therapist burden the client with his/her own difficulties or problems. Psychotherapy, however, provides an unusually safe situation in which the problems of everyday intimacy can be revealed, and solutions discovered. It requires a genuineness and mutuality on both sides, as it is only in 'real' situations that new ways of tackling difficulties can be learnt.

The conversation needs to be developed at the right pace. Ideally it should be progressed in a step-wise fashion. The steps must be the right height. The pace should allow a person to remain in touch with feelings and bodily experiences, without creating so much anxiety that the person cuts off and blocks. In this therapy, the manner in which steps are taken is more important than the content of the conversation. Discoveries are made in the actual 'act' of relating, not in talking about a problem.

Doing no harm

The most important consideration for any psychotherapist is to do no harm. Therapy can be life-changing, or it can alleviate unbearable distress, or it can be moderately helpful, or of no help at all. It should not, however, be harmful. The techniques described above that constitute a Conversational Model of therapy if used inappropriately, or over-zealously or incompetently, are capable of causing harm to the client who is being seen. The pace at which therapy moves, the timing of interventions, knowing when and when not to encourage someone to stay in the 'here and now', are all things that can only be learnt through supervision, and meticulous self-scrutiny via the help of audio recordings.

Therapists will make mistakes. Mistakes in themselves are not bad things, and they are a normal feature of most relationships. If mistakes can be repaired, the therapeutic relationship can often be stronger, as a result of the reparative process. It is a mark of experienced and skilful therapists that they can address and repair ruptures in the therapeutic relationship (Aspland et al., 2008; Stiles et al., 2004a). Many aspects of the Conversational Model encourage the restoration of the therapeutic relationship if some form of dissonance has occurred. Negotiation, basing interventions on cues, working in the 'here and now', and the use of 'I and we' are all techniques, which if used naturally, help the therapist to address misunderstandings or moments of conflict which occur with a client.

However, therapists must be aware of common potential dangers and pitfalls when practising psychotherapy – any form of psychotherapy. In a seminal paper entitled 'The Persecutory Therapist', Meares and Hobson (1977) outlined some of the key ways in which the therapist can unintentionally be drawn into several different kinds of damaging behaviours.

Intrusion

In some therapies, this can occur when the therapist is too probing and asks too many questions in an interrogative manner. Such questioning should be unlikely in the Conversational Model, but therapists can also be too intuitive, and even if correct, can propel the disclosure for the client at a pace which is too fast and too exposing for him/her to bear. As discussed earlier, the therapist can be quite active in encouraging the client to re-experience difficult feelings, but, in extremes, it can feel to the client as if the therapist has invaded his/her mind.

The Conversational Model is a collaborative enterprise in which the client must feel safe, and only disclose or share personal information when he/she wishes to. Hobson's idea of aloneness-togetherness is particularly appropriate in this context. All people need an 'inner-space' which is theirs and theirs alone, and a 'space-between' which can be shared with others (Hobson, 1985: 201). The importance of picking up cues from the client to guide the therapist's interventions cannot be emphasised too strongly.

Derogation

This occurs when in subtle ways the client is made to feel patronised, 'bad' or 'ill'. Some aspects of traditional psychotherapy theory include terms that can seem derogatory and denigrating, whether by using a diagnosis to pin someone down rather than act as a reference point, or by the use of 'clever' technical language making the other person feel inadequate or stupid. In these examples, there is a failure to understand the client from the client's own perspective. In subtle ways the client is made to feel inferior to the therapist.

Invalidation of experience

One of the most damaging things a therapist can do is to disaffirm what the client thinks and believes. This again can arise from a false understanding of traditional psychotherapy theory. The therapist assumes that the client does not mean what he or she thinks and the 'real' meaning is being blocked. In this scenario, the therapist is always right as, if the client tries to disagree, it can be labelled crudely as 'resistance'. In the Conversational Model, the therapist's job is to amplify the client's feeling, and to extend awareness, not to dispute it.

In their paper, Hobson and Meares did not try to explain why these 'persecutory' dynamics occur, although they give a vivid account of how things can escalate into a persecutory spiral. They are drawing attention to the inevitability that even the best therapists will at least occasionally fall into the trap of being unhelpful. They stress that the therapist's job is not to be perfect, but to be able to listen actively for evidence that they have got something wrong. The client may acquiesce rather than explore further; they may talk about a parallel situation where an outside figure (dentist, tax inspector, traffic warden, thoughtless driver) is used to allude to the hurt being caused.

Very little has been written or acknowledged about the potentially harmful aspects of psychological therapy, although it is achieving greater recognition. PI therapy is one of the few approaches that acknowledged this problem, with specific guidance about what and what not to do in any therapeutic situation.

Summary

In the last three chapters, the main components of PI therapy have been described. The different competencies should be used seamlessly to create a process of sharing and collaborating to facilitate interpersonal problem-solving. In this form of therapy, the development of the relationship between the client and the therapist is the key to revealing problems and difficulties in the client's interpersonal relationships, and it is also the main vehicle through which change occurs.

The following three chapters will discuss in much greater detail how the model is used in practice, going through from the beginning of a therapy, through the work of the middle sessions and coming to a creative ending.

PART II

PRACTITIONER MANUAL

SECTION B: APPLYING THE SKILLS

7

The Initial Sessions

Introduction

The second section of this practitioner manual comprises three chapters (7–9) that describe the application of the competencies in the overall process of a course of brief therapy, including the initial, intermediate and final phase of therapy. The chapters include practical advice about how to structure the process, how to start a session of therapy, building theoretical models, using goodbye letters, and ending. More experienced therapists may wish to pass quickly through parts of these chapters as some of what will be said is generic to all therapies, although the notion of deliberate practice would suggest that these generic skills benefit from continual practice. However, the main emphasis in keeping with the PI model is to use these strategies to deepen the *feeling language* between therapist and client, as will be discussed further in Chapter 8. The present chapter will focus on starting therapy and the initial sessions.

The framework, settings, and facilitating conditions

Each session of therapy usually lasts for 45 to 50 minutes, but, whatever time is available, the length of the sessions is agreed at the beginning of therapy and normally remains the same for the duration of therapy. It is preferable that the client and therapist meet on a weekly basis, at the same time and on the same day each week. If changes to this structure do need to be made, they become part of the ongoing conversation between the therapist and client.

This formal structure is important as it provides a sense of security and reliability for the client. It also enables any changes in the routine of therapy to be easily identified. These can sometimes be the first indication of significant emotional tensions between the client and therapist. For example, a client who feels angry or disappointed with his/her therapist may not tell the therapist directly but may start coming late to the therapy sessions. This is more evident when the scheduling of the sessions in terms of time is the same.

Box 7.1   Structure of brief PI therapy

Brief therapy

1. Initial sessions

a.   The audio recording and supervision
b.   Settling in
c.   The problem
d.   Plan of treatment
e.   Link symptom development to interpersonal difficulties
f.   Therapeutic alliance
g.   Theoretical model and formulation

2. Intermediate sessions

a.   Active exploration of the problem
b.   Attend to moments of change
c.   Testing solutions
d.   Building an explanatory model
e.   Passivity to activity
f.   Deepening of a feeling language
g.   Personal conversation and symbolic transformation

3. Final sessions

a.   Explicit discussion of ending
b.   Link ending to previous loss/dilemmas re intimacy
c.   Review the main problem
d.   Review significant changes
e.   Review how work can be continued by the client although therapy will end
f.   Involve client in the development and production of a farewell letter
g.   Say goodbye

An example of how brief therapy is structured is shown in Box 7.1 and the elements are covered in this chapter and in the following two chapters. It is important that the therapist structures each session of therapy. Important information (e.g. the therapist going on holiday) is best discussed at the start of a session and it is often helpful to let the client know when the session is approaching the last few minutes, particularly if the client is distressed.

It is the nature of therapy that significant issues often emerge towards the end of sessions. Therapy is not only about helping people to express feelings; it is also about helping them to contain difficult feelings. Handling the ending of sessions needs particular skill and tact, which is gained through practice and experience. In brief, if the client is experiencing difficulty ending the session, these examples show how a therapist can structure the end of each session, see the parallels with managing feelings on a larger scale (such as the end of a relationship), make tentative guesses about how the client is feeling and help to guide the client towards ways of using structure to manage difficult feelings from the past.

Certain factors are common to most therapies. Although these factors may be non-specific, they are often extremely important and help the therapy to run smoothly. These include warmth, friendliness, supportiveness and empathy. The purpose of these factors is to facilitate an understanding of what the client is experiencing and try to develop a sense of feelings being shared between the client and therapist. Empathic understanding is particularly important in the PI model. However, there is an interesting conundrum captured by Robert Hobson: 'How dull life would be if we all had accurate empathy – there would be nothing left to correct. Therapy is about the correction of misunderstandings' (personal communication, circa 1980). So therapy is about the process of trying to understand the client, but not always getting it right.

It is important for all inexperienced therapists to receive regular supervision from a therapist who is trained and experienced. This can be on a one-to-one basis or in a small group setting. Psychotherapy cannot be learnt just from a manual. It is a skill that is acquired through closely supervised practice. We recommend that all psychotherapy sessions are audio recorded (provided the client gives permission – usually in writing); that the therapist listens to all sessions of the therapy; and that audio recordings of sessions are played for at least part of each supervision session as they provide a clear focus on the experience of the therapy and the interactions between the therapist and client. The atmosphere of supervision should be collegial and not hierarchical, with the more experienced therapist acting as supervisor; providing a form of 'scaffolding' to help the therapist gain understanding and perspective as effectively as possible. In a group setting the other therapists in training, when adding their perspective, can not only assist the therapist presenting but also internalise the model using a different form of learning.

The first five minutes

A lot can happen in the first five minutes of therapy. It will involve the initial greeting of the client and a meeting of two people, previously unknown to each other. Hobson noted the importance of the initial handshake or greeting, noting the information held in the type of handshake offered by the client. Although small, his point was simple: a handshake or greeting is one of the initial contributions to the conversation, a minute particular, which provides information for the therapist within the initial few seconds of meeting.

The therapist may have received detailed information about the client in the form of a referral letter, or there may be a therapy questionnaire that the client has completed, or the therapist may know nothing at all about the client. Hobson preferred not to have any prior information about the person he would see as he would say, 'I want to know them. I don't want to know "about" them.' He was also concerned that his judgement may be biased or altered by hearing other people's concerns about the person he was about to meet.

It is difficult for therapists to see clients without receiving information about them and gathering information to help record any risks. However, the main purpose of the first session is still for the therapist to try to know something *of* the client, rather than know a lot of things *about* him or her.

So, how to start a session? Try to put yourself in the position of the client, waiting in a waiting room, feeling anxious, waiting to meet a 'therapist/counsellor', maybe with all kinds of mixed-up thoughts and feelings about why you are there. Never forget just how anxiety-provoking this may be. Make sure when you greet your client for the first time you are warm, welcoming and sincere. Say clearly who you are, greet them, with an offer to shake their hand if that is culturally appropriate, and show them to your room. Try to speak to them as you both walk to the room. Try to avoid a forbidding silence.

Be aware of anything and everything they do or say. Therapy has already begun. It is your job to look after your client. This involves making sure they are seated in a comfortable fashion, their belongings are safe, their coat is hanging up, you won't be disturbed, the room is conducive to *disclosure and intimacy.* That is, ensure there is no harsh or flickering fluorescent lighting, chairs placed at an angle to each other so that making and breaking eye contact is natural, they have water and tissues available, and they can see a clock. Identifying shared sight of a clock is crucial – it is not a device to have behind the client so that only the therapist can see it. If the client cannot see the time and is too anxious to make overt use of their own watch, then at best their attention will be distracted and at worse they will feel lost in time. The aim of the therapist is to put all of your energy and empathy towards trying to understand and help the client in the next 50 minutes such that they feel able to return for the next session.

The audio recorder and supervision

Your client may have already been informed that the sessions will be audio recorded, either at their psychotherapy assessment or during the referral process, or they may know nothing. You need to explain the purpose of recording the sessions, how you will safeguard the client's identity and personal information, who will have access to the recordings and how the recordings will be stored securely. You will also need to obtain signed consent in most settings, and we think this is good practice. You will also need to inform the client about whatever supervision is in place.

It is our experience that the vast majority of people do not have a problem with the sessions being audio recorded or with the therapist receiving supervision. However, the example below is of a client who does have some initial misgivings.

Box 7.2 Explaining audio recording and gaining consent

THERAPIST: Before we go any further, I must explain the recorder. As you can see there's a machine here and a microphone. I will use this to record our sessions. It's normal and good practice in psychotherapy. It enables me to listen to the time we have spent together again, to see if there are things I have missed,...and it generally helps me to be able to help you...a bit more. I also meet with three colleagues for what's called supervision, where we discuss the clients we are seeing and I may play parts of the tape, if I think it will be of help. My colleagues will not know your name or be given any information that would identify you. I'd like to stress again that this is good practice and it's like quality control. I realise it's quite a bit to take in...

CLIENT: It's a bit off-putting. Who are these colleagues?

THERAPIST: Yes...it is off-putting...but most people settle and get used to it...but for this treatment...important I spend time...to our discussions... as well as meeting with you. The colleagues...there are three of them...they are all psychotherapists/counsellors. They all work in this department. If you want their names, I'm happy to tell you.

CLIENT: Umh...what happens to the recordings.

THERAPIST: Recordings are password protected [include the employing organisation's policies], and I use a code to identify them, so no one knows your identity. At the end of the therapy, I will erase them... or...well sometimes...people ask for them...and if you wanted them...we could talk about that. Also...sometimes...people like to listen to the sessions themselves...and again we could talk about that...if you wanted.

CLIENT: I'm not sure...if I would want to do that.

THERAPIST: No...ok....do you have any other questions...anything else you are not sure about?

CLIENT: No.

THERAPIST: Ok...I need to ask you to sign a consent form. This states that I have explained all those things to you and that you consent to it?

CLIENT: What would happen if I didn't give consent.

THERAPIST: That would be ok, we would still meet, but I wouldn't be able to listen to the sessions...and in this kind of treatment...that's quite an important part...You sound as if you are not sure.

CLIENT: No...I am ok with it...it makes sense.

As you will see from the above transcript, clients may sometimes want to listen to sessions themselves. In most circumstances, in brief therapy, we think this is helpful and it can result in some significant steps forward. It is, however, important to discuss each arrangement regarding recording in supervision before any agreement is reached. There may be a variety of reasons why the client asks for recordings of the sessions and it is important in PI therapy to try to understand the reasons underlying the client's request. Is it that the client is frightened of missing something? Are there hidden reasons why the client may want to have recordings? What will the client do with the recordings?

Whilst there may be some concerns that the client may over-analyse portions of the therapy, or focus on one small fragment of conversation, which may or may not be helpful, the likely benefits probably outweigh any potential harm. In the health sphere, it is becoming more common for patients to record their contacts with doctors, and all therapists should be mindful that it is possible with modern technology for any client to audio record any session of therapy. This is a relatively under-researched area of therapy, and all cases are different. What is important is that any variation from the normal practice should be carefully thought about and discussed in supervision.

Settling in

The client has had a lot to deal with in the first few moments of meeting. He/she has sat down in a strange room, with a stranger, and most likely with an audio recorder. How might the therapist respond to this situation? An example is shown in Box 7.3.

Box 7.3   Settling in

THERAPIST: I reckon it all feels a bit strange...to come here...see someone... like me...and the recorder...

A statement as in Box 7.3 often helps to ease anxiety and help settle the client so he or she can relax a little better. This step is crucial as it is not helpful to expect people to talk about themselves if they feel ill at ease and wary. Many people are very fearful of seeking therapeutic help. They may feel they have been told to come by their doctor, they may not see any value to it, or they may be quite hopeful it will be of help. A statement like the one above allows these things to be openly discussed. The therapist should be making every effort to tune in to how the client is behaving and feeling in these opening moments, via verbal and non-verbal cues.

The problem

In this model of therapy, we start with the client's main problem and try to get a shared understanding of the client's experience. At this stage we are not interested in facts about the problem such as how long it has been troubling the client or when it started. We want to focus on the problem (i.e. the experience) itself. The problem may be any of the following: an intense worry about something, a headache that won't go away, dizzy spells, feeling low, chronic tummy pains, a recent self-harm episode, no energy, etc. Whatever the problem, the job of the therapist is to stay with the problem and explore it.

Box 7.4   Focusing on the problem

THERAPIST: It's not easy to begin; some things are difficult to put into words. Perhaps we could start if you could say something about what you would most like help with…right now. [Emphasise this word]

Features of the model that help the therapist explore the nature of the problem include: making statements, understanding hypotheses, 'here and now', negotiating style, and using 'I' and 'we' as discussed in earlier chapters. Box 7.5 is an example from the beginning of a therapy session.

Box 7.5   The first five minutes of a therapy session

[*Note: Bracketed, italic text indicates the model competencies.*]

CLIENT: I hope I can answer your questions.

THERAPIST: Umh.

CLIENT: I hope I can answer your questions.

THERAPIST: Well we'll go into that shortly…it's not so much what I want to know but I'm hoping to help you say the things you want to say… [*Statement*]

CLIENT: Sometimes I can, but sometimes I can be…lost for words.

THERAPIST: So can I. We all can… When we are talking about things like feelings it's very hard to put words onto them. [*I and we; Statement*]

CLIENT: Yes…it's hard to let go.

THERAPIST: I suggest we settle down a bit first.

CLIENT: Yes…

THERAPIST: I can imagine…you're pretty much on edge…[*Understanding hypothesis*]

(Continued)

(Continued)

CLIENT: Umh…all the time…more so now…

THERAPIST: It's a strange situation…we'll have 45 minutes, so we'll finish on the hour. There's a clock on the side so you can see the time, so you know how long we have so you won't be left high and dry…But let's look if we can have a look at how you are now…you said it's how you normally feel but a bit more so…[*Focus on feelings*]

CLIENT: No I can get worse than I am now…I'm not too bad now, considering what I'm doing…everything seems to hit me later on unless I try to block it out completely…Even a telephone call…will hit me later…but even now I'm just trying to really block it all out.

THERAPIST: I suppose what you're saying is…Look what happens here might be all very well but it might hit me when I get outside that door. [*Understanding hypothesis*]

CLIENT: It will hit me…er…oh I'll give you another example. If I hear something upsetting, I'll just try and block it out. I don't know how to explain it.

THERAPIST: But it might happen if you discover something about you…it might hit you afterwards. So you are saying it's up to me, and it is in a way, to have that in mind. [*Understanding hypothesis*]

CLIENT: Yes…umh…

THERAPIST: But in this interview you don't have to put things in the right way…we can wander around…

CLIENT: I'll tend to do that to you. Sometimes I get straight to the point. Sometimes I can't answer at all. I say what I think. Sometimes I can't say anything at all.

THERAPIST: I would like to start if you could say something about what you would most like help with right now. [*Focus on feelings*]

CLIENT: Right now.

THERAPIST: Right now, here and in your life at the moment. [*Focus on feelings*]

CLIENT: I've got that much tension, stuff inside my brain…when I start to have a fainting or a dizzy spell or go off balance…that frustrates me a lot. I want that to stop.

THERAPIST: Well let us stay with that…I'm not sure I heard all your words…(yes) but I heard the word at the end 'off balance'. [*Focus on feelings, Therapist picks up a potential 'Living Symbol'*]

CLIENT: Off balance…I get this off-balance feeling…I start to feel uneasy… it could get worse than that…I have lost my balance completely for nine months.

THERAPIST: And fall down? [*Understanding hypothesis*]

CLIENT:	I don't let it get to that stage, because I sit down before that happens or it completely changes...I...er get faint but I don't go right out to it...I have all the symptoms of faint, I feel numb, horrible but I don't completely go out to it. That's another side to me...I get quite a few different symptoms.
THERAPIST:	Umh...
CLIENT:	Umh...That's just one side of me...but the symptoms irritate me, I've got a few phobias but these symptoms irritate me a lot.
THERAPIST:	Umh...well perhaps we could stay with this. [*Focus on feelings*]
CLIENT:	All right.
THERAPIST:	The feeling as far as I've got it so far [right] ...you might feel faint [yes], you might feel unsure of yourself...with this comes a fear? [*Understanding hypothesis*]
CLIENT:	Yes it is a fear, yes.
THERAPIST:	That you might fall? [*Understanding hypothesis*]
CLIENT:	Yes, yes, because you feel that off balance...you know...I suppose it comes down to I might fall, yes right and I don't want to fall.
THERAPIST:	We can talk can't we about off balance...we can talk about it in a bodily way like falling down or we can talk about the balance of the mind and you might be also scared that somehow that you can't get your thoughts in order. [*Beginning of an explanatory hypothesis*]
CLIENT:	The thoughts...how can I explain that...when I do feel like that I feel uneasy and I don't know what to...and if I'm laying down I don't feel safe at all.
THERAPIST:	Not safe? [*Focus on feeling*]
CLIENT:	No, I'd not feel safe at all. I like to know my feet are touching the ground (sits with feet on ground and holds chair with both hands). I like to be firm. So I what I do is sit very still and I hope I don't have to lay down and if I do have to lie down I can only lay on one side. This side here [indicating left side] is completely out...I have to lie on this right side.
THERAPIST:	If you lie on your left side? [Indicates left side]
CLIENT:	No if I lie on my right I feel a lot safer than if I lie on my left.
THERAPIST:	If you lie on your left? [Mirrors actions of client]
CLIENT:	I don't feel safe at all. Especially when things like that happen to me......You're going to ask me why.
THERAPIST:	No I'm not...I'm not...I'm wondering if you get any different sensations from the different sides. [*Focus on feeling*]

(Continued)

(Continued)

CLIENT: Yes I do. [Sits forward] I feel I've got full control of this side of my body [points to right side] [therapist leans forward]. This side here [gestures to left side] seems to be a lot weaker. Yes even sitting here now I can feel I'm a lot stronger in this half of me. This side of me just follows, it's useless. For some reason...I feel...I mean...everything works.

THERAPIST: Umh.

CLIENT: And the balance feeling, even when I lie in bed I'm so tired by lying on this side [left side] I turn over...like everybody does...and I start to feel sick and very uneasy so I quickly have to turn back.

THERAPIST: Are you right handed?

CLIENT: Yes. I am right handed. That confuses me.

THERAPIST: Umm...ummh...Umm...your left side...sounds to me if it's a more... sort of unknown side. [*Understanding hypothesis*]

CLIENT: It is an unknown side. You're right.

THERAPIST: Do you know we sometimes speak of the sinister side of ourselves as at the left side, as if it's dark and unknown. [*Beginning of an explanatory hypothesis*]

CLIENT: Right...for example just before I came in I was just mucking about... don't know why...because I tend to be on the serious side because I've been ill for so long and I threw my leg up [lifts right leg] and this leg goes up quite all right but this leg [pointing to left leg] I couldn't get it as high...no matter how much I tried. I don't know if that's unusual. [Therapist mirrors client's movements with his legs as though trying out how it feels]

THERAPIST: Umh...I'm not sure if you are scared whether there might be something really wrong with your body or not.

CLIENT: I'm very confused at this point. I keep saying to myself there has to be something wrong for me to be like this. And they say to me. 'It's all nerves. You're unhappy.' But would unhappiness do all this to me. I'm very confused. And no one seems to be giving me any answers.

THERAPIST: Well let's see if we can get at least an approach...we're not going to get the answer...But at least we might look at what things we might explore. Yeah? [*Beginning of exploratory therapy rationale*]

The example in Box 7.5 illustrates how hard the therapist works to explore and stay with the main problem by focusing on feelings. In this case the client uses the term 'off balance'. The therapist picks this up. The feeling is associated with a fear of falling. This moves to a feeling of not being safe. The client then describes this unusual experience of not feeling safe if she lies on her left side. She then describes a weakness on her left side. The therapist suggests the left side of her is 'unknown'. The client agrees. There is a stepwise movement occurring between the therapist and client as the problem is explored. The therapist draws on some theoretical knowledge about the left being the 'sinister' side, but that is not picked up by the client and not pursued further.

The first five minutes of a session of therapy often contain key interactions between the therapist and client, which will resonate throughout the whole therapeutic endeavour. There are many interesting and revealing exchanges in the above example, which would merit lengthy discussion and consideration in supervision. Of most importance is that the client has felt understood and that her symptoms have been taken seriously. There are the beginnings of a therapeutic bond and a collaboration to try to explore her problems in more detail.

Plan of treatment

It is the therapist's task always to be aware of the time and to structure the time accordingly. Towards the end of the first session, the therapist should try to draw together the experiences that have been shared with the client in the first session and if possible develop *an exploratory therapy rationale* (an example of this has already been given in Chapter 6).

The therapist should set out a plan of meetings over the next few weeks. If it is a very brief therapy (e.g. four sessions) it is best to set dates for each of the meetings so the client is clear about the planned meetings. If the therapy is 16 sessions, then the therapist should give an approximate estimate of the likely finish point (for example, 'So we will meet for 16 sessions, so we will probably finish some time in July.').

Finally it is helpful to end the first session by saying something warm and positive about the meeting. This must be spoken from the heart, so it is best only to say something if it is genuinely meant: 'Well...it's been very nice to meet with you...I think we've made a start...I will look forward to seeing you again.'

Linking symptoms to interpersonal difficulties

The aim of the initial sessions is to continue to develop the conversation in a similar fashion to the first session. By tentatively suggesting hypotheses, the therapist is hoping to promote dialogue, a dialogue involving inner feelings, and a sharing of experiences from which meanings begin to form and links to relationships emerge. There is a repeated process of *sequencing of events* (see Chapters 1 and 6) so that patterns and forms emerge. Warded-off or avoided feelings begin to be tolerated and with that comes new possibilities of changing previous maladaptive patterns of behaviour.

During this process the therapist will learn a lot about the client's symptom history and interpersonal relationships. The *about*, however, is not as important as what is experienced and brought alive in the session. In the next example in Box 7.6 the client is talking about problems with her husband and particularly the difficulties she has getting on with her stepson. The therapist focuses on her feelings and by doing this she is able to disclose the hatred she feels for him and her fears that he will think she is a monster. This example is from a session with the same client as discussed previously who had feelings of being 'off balance'. At the end of the section in Box 7.6, the therapist makes a link between her feelings of hatred for her stepson and her feelings of being 'off balance'. He is using the term to denote both physical feelings and off balance as in emotional balance.

Box 7.6 Link symptoms to interpersonal difficulties

THERAPIST: And you said earlier that your husband didn't understand you.

CLIENT: No, but he didn't want to.

THERAPIST: I mean there are a lot of problems between you two.

CLIENT: Yes because he's said to me, if you treat my son better, I'll treat you better.

THERAPIST: Sounds to me as if he treats you badly.

CLIENT: He can do. He can be very nice but he can also be…treat me badly… And I found he had got very distant…we because I can't be nicer to his son as he puts it. It's his guilt not mine.

THERAPIST: Uh.

CLIENT: He said to me you are not a proper mother to him. Meaning loving him. Oh I dress him and feed him.

THERAPIST: I suppose there must be…you haven't got the sense of the feelings for your stepson, as for the others. [*Understanding hypothesis*]

CLIENT: I haven't. I can admit it to you.

THERAPIST: To me. [*I and we*]

CLIENT: Yes to you. But I couldn't say it to my husband as he would just pick up and walk out, and use that as an excuse.

THERAPIST: Uh.

CLIENT: And use that as an excuse. He knows deep down that there is something there. I do feed him, dress him very well. I do a lot of things for him but he hates the fact I don't love him. He expected me to love him from the word go and I'm not the type of person like that – I need time. I don't like to be pushed…so things got a lot worse.

THERAPIST: I was wondering whether sometimes you get worried about your feelings about your stepson. [*Focus on feelings*]

CLIENT:	I do.
THERAPIST:	I mean, I wonder if you get mad with him sometimes. [*Focus on feelings*]
CLIENT:	I do...I do all of the time. I won't deny it. I'm angry with him all the time.
THERAPIST:	Yes well...let us have a look at that. [Sits forward. Uses hands to gesture a focus]. Stay with that (...all right...). You feel your husband doesn't understand and you were scared when you came in here that I wouldn't understand. [*Linking hypothesis*]
CLIENT:	No...ok I accept...
THERAPIST:	Now you sound as if you have to reassure me a bit. The thing is not to give me what you think I want but for me to try to understand what you are feeling. Now you say you feel angry with him the whole time. [*Understanding hypothesis*]
CLIENT:	Yes I blame him...because I'm blaming a child but I should blame my husband really which I'll do but I can forgive my husband when...he is nice to me, but I can't forgive my stepson.
THERAPIST:	Because it's really his fault? [*Understanding hypothesis*]
CLIENT:	I blame my stepson yes...very much because he did come into my life and my life did go down from that point. I wasn't that healthy before that but I could cope with a lot of things. But I wasn't on tablets but I feel he has changed my life completely for the worst. Not for the better. For the worst. I do have a strong hatred for him. But I wouldn't hurt him. I wouldn't do that.
THERAPIST:	No...I wasn't saying that. We're staying with the feeling. [*Focus on feeling*]
CLIENT:	That is the feeling.
THERAPIST:	And you...you feel...you get mad with him. [*Focus on feeling*]
CLIENT:	I do now but at first I didn't – he used to walk all over me and I didn't like that at all. I do feel awful afterwards.
THERAPIST:	Could you say something about how you feel afterwards.
CLIENT:	I feel guilty...I think he must feel I am a monster but I don't feel that at the time. At the time I don't care because I am so angry.
THERAPIST:	You feel that he must feel that you are a monster. [*Understanding hypothesis*]
CLIENT:	Yes...yes I do feel guilty that when he grows up and looks back he's going to really hate me. It does worry me. But as soon as I see him I start getting very bitter.

(Continued)

(Continued)

THERAPIST: It isn't easy is it to be hated or to hate. [*Understanding hypothesis*]

CLIENT: No.

THERAPIST: But it's very strong…isn't it. [*Focus on feeling*]

CLIENT: Very strong. I've tried to be nice but I can't. The less I say to him the better it is for me.

THERAPIST: And as I hear it there are times when you almost feel that he's responsible for your troubles…For your being off balance. [*Beginning of explanatory hypothesis*]

CLIENT: I've never been right…since then. I've never been well.

This interview is the start of an exploration of her symptoms and the links to her conflictual feelings about her stepson and her husband.

The therapeutic alliance

The strength of the bond between the client and therapist is an important determinant of the overall outcome of therapy. Many of the individual components of the PI model, if used competently, help foster a close bond between the client and therapist. *Negotiating, picking up cues, using a language of mutuality* and most of all *sharing experience* in a close and safe relationship strengthen the therapeutic alliance. Therapists will get things slightly wrong, they will miss certain cues, or they may push things slightly too far. What is important is that therapists recognise these mistakes, acknowledge them and work hard to correct them – the correction of misunderstandings – in order to re-adjust and re-align themselves with the client. The mistakes should not be catastrophic as, within the model, we are looking for small steps forward. Suggestions made in a tentative manner can be corrected, withdrawn, re-worded, and re-fashioned if they are not helpful.

The theoretical model and formulation

Chapter 1 described the theoretical background to the model, which is rooted in the domain of the interpersonal. The main approach involves helping the client to find ways to manage and share warded off feelings and difficulties. This involves developing a 'feeling language', a way of conversing which allows feelings to be brought alive and images, memories, symbols to be shared with the therapist.

There are differing approaches to formulation among experienced therapists using this model. We would suggest that what is important is that there is a shared understanding between the therapist and client as to what is the main problems are, and how this can be addressed in therapy. Formulations are important as all people strive to make sense of themselves and their lives. The priority in PI therapy, however, is that the formulation arises from the *shared feeling* between the client and therapist and not from an intellectual process. In PI therapy the formulations that develop have a tendency to start as *micro* in scale in that they arise from a focus on the *minute particulars*. These micro understandings are slowly brought together so the client forms a more coherent meta-understanding of his/her self. One can liken this process perhaps to seeing a painting close up. You see only the brush strokes and parts of an image. These small parts may begin to form a kind of patchwork with more and more pieces linking together until finally you appreciate the whole canvas. Even when the canvas is seen as a whole, it is multi-layered and complex, from which shifting meanings and emotions emerge. What is of most importance in this process of understanding or model forming is not the eventual model alone, but *how* it was developed.

Through this process a *working model* begins to be shared with the client and the development of this early constellation of ideas has a function that is broadly similar to a formulation. It can be written down, as we show later in the chapter, but its primary function is not intended to be a static statement of how things are but a tentative working version from which therapist and client can move forward.

There has been a lot of discussion across relational therapies about how change comes about. Work with the assimilation model suggests assimilation of warded-off experiences result in a change in the self that becomes more cohesive and coherent. When PI therapy is used in an intensive long-term format, there is much greater focus upon the self, but even in brief therapy, changes to the self frequently occur. Theoretical constructs in relation to the self and the role of PI therapy in reparative treatment of the self are discussed further by Meares (2012b). The assimilation model (Stiles et al., 1990) suggests that the repetitive cycling through problems gradually allowing a deeper understanding is characteristic of this type of relational learning where warded-off experiences gradually emerge into awareness in a painful way and then are gradually processed until the client finds tentative solutions and eventually mastery of the difficulty.

Using the examples in Boxes 7.5 and 7.6 we demonstrate how the fragments can be pulled together to form a more working formulation. The client and therapist begin to develop a series of micro-models:

- The client describes a coping strategy of trying to block out things she finds upsetting.
- A link is made between a physical feeling of being 'off balance' and a fear of falling.

- There are 'two sides' to the client in her experience and the several possible meanings of this phrase are held in mind.
- The left side is an unknown and unsafe side.
- The client describes two ways in which her husband treats her (nicely and badly).
- The client feels her husband doesn't understand her. There is a possible link to a fear that the therapist may not understand her either.
- The client finds it difficult to love her stepson; more than that, she hates him and treats him badly and fears that he will think she is a monster.
- There may be a link between her problems with symptoms and the problematic feelings she has for her stepson.
- She has begun to get in touch with feelings that normally she would try to block out – like hatred for her stepson – while in the session with the therapist.

As the therapy progresses, more pieces of the jigsaw will be added, so a more coherent overall picture is realised. The therapist draws together some of the *micro* models into a larger model when developing an *exploratory rationale*. In the example discussed, the therapist goes on to draw a connection between the client's physical symptoms of shutting down and a fear of losing control and becoming very angry. He draws a connection between her body and mind, and suggests that just as the left side of her body feels 'unknown' to her, there is a side of her mind that is also unknown. He suggests this dark side could contain frightening things, feelings she cannot face. He also suggests, in keeping with the model, that it is more important to get in touch with 'these difficult feelings' so they are no longer warded off, than it is to have an intellectual explanation about her symptoms or feelings.

One perhaps can see how many of the above *micro-models* may coalesce together to form a coherent story about this client's life. There is a persistent theme of opposites – good and bad: her father and husband are both described as loving and angry people. The client describes herself as having two sides.

A memory from childhood, which the client talks about later in the therapy, becomes very important. She remembers the first time she felt 'off balance' was when her normally loving mother became unexpectedly and inexplicably angry with her (see Box 7.5). Her mother had returned home from hospital, after giving birth to a new baby. The client described that her mother was seated in the living room of their house, surrounded by family, with the new baby on her lap. The client remembered entering the room and immediately sensing that she was not wanted and that her mother was angry with her. She was thrown 'off balance'. The feeling of 'off balance' now came to be understood as being linked to this key event, when the client felt shocked by her mother's anger, and she felt that she was not wanted, and that the new baby was preferred to her.

Maybe the client felt she was no longer loved? Maybe she shut off from this sense of loss in relation to her mother, and her consequent anger about being abandoned? Maybe she coped by pushing feelings out of awareness, creating an experience of having 'two sides' to herself? Maybe this way of coping worked until the client married and she then had to care for his child? She, once again, had to face a 'new child' – her stepson – coming into the home. The parallels between this situation and the scenario she described as a child when her mother brought home a new baby are quite striking.

There were many more interweaving links and patterns in the above therapy, particularly ones involving feeling rejected and angry, and the client's tendency to try to please people to avoid any forms of confrontation, or any possibility that would lead to anger.

As the conversation developed, the sense of coherence became stronger and the requirement for feelings and fears to be warded off became less strong. Perhaps what is most important is that the client experienced a change in the experience of self. Her previously unknown, uncontrollable left side that caused her to be off balance began to be seen as an aspect of herself. What was dark and unknown and sinister has begun to be known and assimilated as the experience of self has been enlarged.

The 'alive' problem in the room

In the PI model, 'the problem' should be manifest in the room at any point in the therapy. By this we mean that the main problems or difficulties the client is experiencing will inevitably be re-enacted in the relationship with the therapist. This may only be evident in very subtle ways, or it may be prominent and overt. Audio recordings of the therapy, which are played in supervision, can help the therapist and supervisor identify 'the problem in the room' and this should theoretically fit with the micro-models the therapist is developing with the client.

In the example in Box 7.5, the client's first words to the therapist are, 'I hope I can answer your questions', which she then repeats. She then goes on to say, 'No I can get worse than I am now...I'm not too bad now, considering what I'm doing...everything seems to hit me later on unless I try to block it out completely...Even a telephone call...will hit me later...but even now I'm just trying to really block it all out.'

We can now see that right at the very beginning of this therapy, the client is showing that she is trying to be helpful to the therapist, to possibly avoid any kind of conflict. The client also talks about having to block things out completely or they 'hit her'. This phrase can now be understood as being a living symbol. Not only does it mean that things will jump out at her unexpectedly, but also that there is a suggestion of violence in the words that she has chosen to use.

Any section of therapy can be used in this fashion for micro study, but the first few minutes of therapy are often very illuminating because of the increased anxiety that is present in any new encounter and it is well worth spending an additional period of time, in micro study of these early interactions.

Summary

This chapter has discussed the initial sessions of a brief PI therapy, with examples to illustrate specific points. Although the model focuses upon the relationship between therapist and client, structure is very important as it provides elements of order, safety, reliability and containment. By the end of the first phase of therapy there should be a 'working model' or formulation to build upon, and refine over the next phase. The following chapter will discuss the intermediate sessions of PI therapy.

8

The Intermediate Sessions

Introduction

This chapter focuses on the middle sessions of a brief course of psychodynamic-interpersonal therapy. By this point, the client and therapist will have agreed an area to work on together and they will have discussed a provisional exploratory rationale and preliminary *working model*. As emphasised earlier, although models are important in helping individual clients develop a sense of meaning and coherence, in PI therapy the greatest emphasis is placed on the process of *developing* a shared model rather than the specific model itself.

Below are the seven key aspects of the middle phase of PI therapy. They often occur interchangeably and simultaneously and in some respects it is somewhat artificial to split them into separate entities. However, for the purposed of a manual, it is easier to describe each aspect separately.

1. Active exploration of the problem
2. Attending to moments of change
3. Testing solutions
4. Building an explanatory model
5. Passivity to activity
6. Deepening of a feeling language
7. Personal conversation and symbolic transformation

1. Active exploration of the problem

The middle sessions of therapy enable the therapist and client to *actively explore* the problem area. The model assumes that one of the most common problems in connecting with others involves approach–avoidance conflict. The client wants to be closer to people but at the same time fears being close. Avoidance is constantly present and is manifest by talking about problems in an abstract *jam-jar* language. The therapist can reinforce this avoidance by talking 'about' the difficulties and so avoiding exploration of them.

Box 8.1   Client and therapist using abstract (jam-jar) language

CLIENT: I think my mother never really loved my father. She picked him because she thought he'd be a good father, but she never showed any affection towards him and basically just treated him like part of the furniture. She always told us to mistrust feelings about people and think with your head. She thought love was a silly emotion and people who fell in love were idiots. I remember her criticising a friend of mine. She was 16 at the time and had a boyfriend. My mum thought it was dreadful. She went on and on about what a slut my friend was. It was the same with things on TV. She would rubbish any films in which there were people who fell in love. She just thought the whole thing was stupid. She didn't get it.

THERAPIST: So she was quite judgemental and critical when it came to love.

In the example in Box 8.1 the therapist continues the conversation with the client *about* the client's mother. A more appropriate response in PI therapy would be for the therapist to try to focus on the client's feelings about her mother. The therapist could have said something like, 'When you describe how your mother behaved, you sound...a bit annoyed...I'm not sure'.

Exploring a difficult problem involves developing a capacity to tolerate anxiety and stress and to stand in 'mysteries, uncertainties, and doubts' (Hobson, 1985: 185). The ideal is a situation of relative safety in which frank and open conversation can develop. Of course, it is unrealistic for the conversation always to be in the *here and now* as the intensity of the therapy would be too great. However, in some therapies most of the conversation between therapist and client may be 'about' something, rather than experiencing feelings in the 'here and now'. A balance between exploration and experiencing in the 'here and now' with time to process and assimilate this kind of experiencing is the ideal scenario.

As discussed in the previous chapter, 'the problem' will be alive and enacted in the therapy room between the client and therapist, even if it is not overtly acknowledged by the therapist or owned by the client. In the example in Box 8.1, the client is ostensibly talking about her mother as someone who mistrusted feelings and thought with her head. She describes her mother denigrating a teenage friend of the client's for having loving feelings towards her boyfriend.

As the client describes this event from her childhood, she is detached and out of touch with her own feelings, and she uses jam-jar language. The client's problem is being enacted in the room and we can hypothesise that the client may be having difficulty in feeling close to the therapist, as such feelings will be inextricably linked to shame and humiliation (and possibly other as yet unknown feelings). The focus of therapy will be to help the client to connect and trust with feelings of closeness towards the therapist (and key others in the client's life), and to overcome the barriers to this, which are so self-evidently present in the example shown. By actually tackling the problem head on in therapy it is often easier then for clients to generalise their experiences to scenarios and relationships in their own lives.

If we look at Box 8.1 again, we can also see that the client talks about her mother not loving her father, and the inference from this is that the client may also have felt unloved by her mother and the product of a loveless union. The therapist in the first example responds to the client by using jam-jar language, the language of the client's mother: The language of reason and of the mind. Even though we are focusing on only one response by the therapist, by staying away from feelings, we can argue that in a micro sense, the therapist has inadvertently played the role of the client's mother.

If the therapist responds using an intervention that picks up feelings, 'When you described how your mother felt...you sounded a bit annoyed', this not only brings feelings into the here and now, but at a micro level it is actually tackling the client's 'problem'. The therapist is in effect saying to the client, 'look feelings are actually really important and it's really important that we try to share them or something of them, rather than doing what your mother did which was to rubbish, avoid and belittle them'.

2. Attending to moments of change

Growth or change in therapy occurs gradually as safety and trust are built up between client and therapist. Change, however, can also occur through steps – moments of insight, when something new happens. It is important that the therapist is attuned and alive to these moments as they are important to build upon, and if recognised can represent pivotal points of change.

Box 8.2   Example of a moment of change

CLIENT: I went for a walk at the weekend with the dogs. I should have known. Got to the park and sat on a bench for a few minutes, then this mad thing came careering over from nowhere and started a fight with Bliss and then Mason joined in. I should have known. I had to drag my two away and eventually it ran off. But I wish I'd never bothered. The idiots round me don't give a **** about their dogs. Just let them run wild.

(Continued)

(Continued)

> Anyway, I thought, *** you, I'm going to let my dogs have a walk...so I stayed out with them...and fortunately nothing else happened.

THERAPIST: As you were telling me this, I was trying to remember how long it's been since you went to the park.

CLIENT: Months...it was last year.

THERAPIST: You were anticipating that something bad was going to happen.

CLIENT: Yes...it always does.

THERAPIST: Yet you went out. You didn't let it put you off and even when that dog came over and attacked your dogs, you still didn't let it put you off.

CLIENT: Well I thought about what you said last week...about being trapped... feeling trapped. It's partly in my own head...I mean I feel like I'm in a prison...in my own house.

THERAPIST: What you did seems to me like a big thing...to go out...to try to sort of break free a bit...and even though...you experienced all that aggro...you stuck with it...

CLIENT: Umh...yes.

THERAPIST: And last week, with me...it sort of felt you had tried to break free a bit...perhaps shared some things with me that you had not spoken about before...or at least for a long time.

CLIENT: I knew you'd bring that up.

THERAPIST: Aarh...errr...Like you were worrying about us talking about it again...

CLIENT: Yes...and...no.

THERAPIST: It's a very big thing for you...to share a secret...a secret like that. A big thing...

CLIENT: I think I'm kinda pleased really.

THERAPIST: But...I wonder if you are also saying to me...look...go carefully... I might feel hurt...or vulnerable...or got at.

CLIENT: Yes...

In the example in Box 8.2, the client had disclosed to the therapist that his father abused him when he was a little boy and later he was raped when he served a prison term for burglary. This represents a stepwise change in the therapy as he had not disclosed such information before and indeed had not been able to tell anyone previously about these experiences. There is a move forward in the therapy and this is also mirrored by a change in the client's behaviour outside of therapy. He takes his dogs for a walk in the park. This is something he has been unable to do for many months because of fears in relation to going out and also low mood. The therapist acknowledges the step forward he has made in a practical sense by daring to go out in the first place and then coping with the dog attack when it occurred.

The therapist also realises the symbolic nature of the communication in that the client is telling him a story about exposure, vulnerability and subsequent attack. The therapist links this back into the therapy and the client's feelings of vulnerability following his disclosure the previous week. Moreover, the client takes an extra step of indicating his conflicting feelings about disclosing and together the client and therapist recognise the need to 'pace' things carefully.

Whenever change occurs in the course of brief therapy, it is important that the therapist acknowledges it and provides support and positive feedback. If possible clients should be encouraged to build upon changes, both within the sessions and in their own lives. Where appropriate such changes can be linked to important therapy conversations and moments of change as shown in the example above.

3. Testing solutions

As the problem becomes clearer and more and more pieces seem to fit together, different ways of responding to feelings and events need to be tried out, both in therapy and outside in the client's world. Change is difficult for all of us, and the therapist must understand how difficult it can be to change even small ways of behaving and how tempting it is to fall back on routine patterns of avoidance.

In the example in Box 8.3, a different client has suffered from depression and anxiety for several years. She is fearful of people and finds it easier to avoid meeting people at all rather than have to interact with them socially. Her father was a very severe, strict man who terrorised her when she was little and she was also terrified of her teachers at school, who frequently used the cane to punish children. Although she was never caned, because she was always good, she lived in fear of punishment.

As the therapy has developed, the client has found it very difficult to stay with feelings but at the same time has shown in a variety of ways that she wants to please the therapist.

Box 8.3   Testing a solution

CLIENT: I try to think about the sessions…you know…in the week…and take on board what you are saying…you know the advice you give.

THERAPIST: I'm not sure…errr…

CLIENT: Oh well…maybe it's not advice…but I think about what you say…you know I do try.

THERAPIST: Yes…I know you are trying…trying very hard…but I wonder if you feel a bit wary of me at times…

(Continued)

(Continued)

CLIENT: I think you've been very nice to me.

THERAPIST: I wonder...although it feels as if you are trying very hard...I also feel...er you feel...you seem...on edge.

CLIENT: No...not really.

THERAPIST: Umh..

CLIENT: I get terrible panics...downstairs...waiting to come up.

THERAPIST: When you are waiting to see me?

CLIENT: Yes...waves of panic and I just want to run away.

THERAPIST: Well...I wonder if you can get in touch with that feeling...as you felt it this morning waiting to see me...but as if it's happening now...and I think it is...just a bit...

CLIENT: It's awful...just dread...sickness...like I'm going to pass out.

THERAPIST: Like you're going to faint...well...can you stay with that feeling...and see what comes to mind.

CLIENT: It's this awful feeling of waiting for my father to come home. Shaking and trembling...trying to hide behind the sofa...hoping he won't see you.

THERAPIST: Try and stay with the feeling if you can.

CLIENT: It's just scary...scared I'll be shouted at again...hit again...terror... praying he won't see me...he'll pick on my sister instead...[long pause]...I hate him...absolutely hate him.

THERAPIST: Yes...and...

CLIENT: I would cheerfully kill him if he wasn't already dead. All the pain and misery he's caused us...all the suffering and he didn't suffer at all. I hate him...he's an absolute...

THERAPIST: Say it.

CLIENT: Bastard. He's an absolute bastard.

Later in the session the therapist makes a link between the fear the client experiences prior to seeing her (the therapist) and the generalised fear the client has towards people, and the fear of her father. The therapist suggests that one way of lessening the fear is to begin to try to face it, and points out that the client has been brave enough to do that with her in the session. In facing her fear, the client has also begun to get in touch with angry and destructive feelings she harbours, and the hatred she feels for her father. These feelings have previously been warded off. The therapist and client have begun to test out possible solutions to her overwhelming fear and panic.

In another example, a client who has suffered from depression and anxiety for many years has begun to explore and share her feelings in the session with the therapist. She has always been a very submissive person who has found it difficult to challenge authority. She has been in an unhappy marriage for years and is dominated by her husband, who she suspects has been having affairs throughout their married life. She works full time, as does he, but she feels responsible for carrying out all the household tasks, and he insists that the home is immaculate. She has been frightened to challenge her husband in case he leaves her.

The therapist and client have explored her fears of abandonment through the imagery of 'having no anchor'. As a small child, her mother was intermittently very ill (she had Crohn's disease) and spent long periods in hospital. During these times, the client had to live with various members of the family (aunties and cousins) as her father did not feel he could work full time and look after her as well.

An early memory from her childhood was one of coming home from school when she was about seven years old to be told by her father that her mother was ill again and she would have to stay with auntie. The feelings associated with this memory were fear and dread at having to stay with auntie, who she didn't like, and also fears that her mum was going to die and she would never see her again.

The client describes feeling empty inside and a terror of being alone. She also begins to share with the therapist angry feelings about being dependent upon her husband. She worries about the therapy ending and fears that she will feel abandoned. She starts to be more assertive with her husband and begins to take small measured steps towards redressing some of the imbalance in their relationship. She faces the possibility he may leave her and begins to wonder why she has been so frightened of this outcome. She begins to acknowledge some of her strengths. In the relationship with the therapist she is noticeably more alive, more connected with her inner self and more connected with the therapist.

4. Building an explanatory model

As the therapy progresses, the client and therapist will continue to develop an understanding of the problem. More and more links will be made between symptoms, feelings and relationships. The therapist needs to hold together the different threads as more and more pieces of the jigsaw are added. It can be helpful for the therapist to summarise from time to time what has been shared and discussed and to try to draw some of the threads together. This can be done in the form of *linking hypotheses, explanatory hypotheses, relating change to therapy* and *patterns in relationships* (see Chapters 5 and 6).

This process in itself can be a helpful learning experience for the client and provides the basis for thinking about change. The therapist should also be thinking about the end of therapy and the farewell letter (see next chapter) and making notes about causal processes or aspects of the model that would be appropriate to include in the letter.

Box 8.4   Building the model

THERAPIST: I suppose...the main thing we've shared is the difficulty you have in trusting people. You immediately assume you will be treated badly and we've talked about your hackles rising even before you meet some in anticipation of how they are going to be.

CLIENT: That's me all over. I'd rather get into a fight...cos I know I'll win.

THERAPIST: ...and it was hard to share things with me...one of things we've talked about is how much initially you talked here, so there was no space almost to feel anything...and the talking was like a big shield. A big shield you held up against me. [Gesturing with hands]

CLIENT: Yes...I do that with everyone.

THERAPIST: But...in the last couple of weeks...you feel different with me...a bit less guarded...you've talked about some important things...but then gone away and worried that I wouldn't want to see you again.

CLIENT: Why would you? No one wants to hear about shit do they? She didn't [meaning mother]. She didn't care what he [father] was doing. She didn't care that we even had food. I had to go across the road to the neighbours to ask if they had anything to eat because there'd be nothing in the house. I'd even steal food if I could find it. I'd only be eight years old.

THERAPIST: That's an awful thing for a little boy to have to cope with and face. There's a kind of linkage however between some of these things... how you were treated by your mum, how you had to fend for yourself from an early age...how you expect people to hurt you...because that's how people treated you when you were little, and perhaps how in someway...you've expected those things of me...to some extent anyway...and you expect them of people who you meet in everyday life...

CLIENT: I know it goes back to them...they screwed me up...[wry smile]...when I was young...it didn't matter. I was so hard... I loved prison...It was safe and...people were scared of me...no one messed with me...

THERAPIST: And being hard...tough...worked for a few years...kept these feelings at bay...but it's all kinda broken down...

CLIENT: Oh yeah...pack of cards...

THERAPIST: Well as we go on...perhaps we'll return to these ideas...keep fitting more things together...to try to make sense of things...the most important thing I think...is for you to be able to face with me... some of these deep fears...you kept at bay...for so long...behind this front of being a really really hard man.

5. Passivity to activity

One of the most important tasks of the therapist is, by his/her responses, to promote a change from passivity to activity (Hobson, 1985: 189). By 'activity' Hobson meant any kind of behaviour that was goal directed. This does not only refer to outward observable movement but also to images, thoughts and emotions over which the client takes ownership of, as opposed to feeling controlled by. The emphasis is on moving from a state of passivity often experienced when distressed or ill to an active state in which the client begins to use the word 'I'. There is a difference between someone who says, 'the illness makes me angry' to someone who says, 'I feel angry'. In this context illness can mean any psychological or physical condition or combination of both regardless of the symptomatology.

Box 8.5   Example of passivity into activity

CLIENT: Ugh…It's completely taken over my life. I don't have a life anymore. I used to be the life and soul of the party, bubbly, full of energy. Now it's just taken over. It just makes me feel so fed up. The pain is so bad in the morning, I have to lie down. It just makes me feel utterly useless.

THERAPIST: Er…you're feeling quite fed up now…as you speak. Can we try and stay with how you are feeling…you feel as if you've lost a part of yourself or who you are…

CLIENT: I…I've lost…who I used to be…I don't feel like anything…like there's anything inside.

---

6. Deepening of a feeling language

Hobson used the term *forms of feeling* for his book about Conversational Model therapy, or PI therapy as we now term it, in a very deliberate way. Hobson drew on the work of Martin Buber who, when commenting on psychotherapy, contrasted what he called 'repair work' with 'the regeneration of an atrophied personal centre', the latter, he suggests, 'can only be attained in the person–person attitude of a partner, not by the consideration and examination of an object' (Buber, 1958: 133). Such a relationship involves a 'feeling language'. The term 'feeling' does not refer to a faculty of emotion as distinct from a faculty of cognition. Rather feeling refers to a form of 'emotional knowing' or 'imaginative, emotion influenced thinking'.

One of the key responsibilities of the therapist in the intermediate sessions of therapy is to deepen the 'feeling language' between client and therapist. This involves trying to stay with feelings and to explore and elaborate symbolic images and metaphors. This is at the heart of PI therapy and is summarised by Hobson (1985: xiii) as follows:

I am concerned with the centre, the basis, of my approach to psychotherapy: a developing relationship. What I say and do in therapy is aimed at promoting understanding:
a 'conversation', a meeting between two experiencing subjects (an I and a Thou), here
and now, in such a way that the learning can be effective in other relationships. If as I
believe, psychotherapy is a matter of promoting a personal dialogue, then we need to
know how to receive, express, and share feeling: how to learn a language of the heart
in its 'minute particulars'.

This process is difficult to convey in a manual but we believe can be enhanced
by close scrutiny and rigorous attention to the audio recordings of therapy sessions. It is by listening to the recordings that the therapist can 'tune in' to the
client, realise when he/she has failed to pick up cues, or responds in a way that
promotes a thinking 'about' rather than 'sharing with'. Russell Meares has used
the term 'empathic resonance' and argues for a priority of value above meaning,
noting that a therapeutic approach that focuses on meaning will differ from that
which gives priority to value: 'Privilege must be given to feeling tones and how
they arise in particular forms of relatedness' (Meares, 2000: 75).

7. Personal conversation and symbolic transformation

A central feature of PI therapy is the promotion of a symbolic attitude, a sort of
expectant waiting, for images, symbols, experiences to emerge from feeling states.
Emotional knowing rarely arises from logical thought processes, especially if
many unacceptable experiences, emotions and thoughts are warded off. Symbols
and metaphor provide a means for visualising the inner world (Meares, 2000:
125). This process of symbolic attention occurs in the context of an interpersonal
relationship and involves a sense of transformative looking which creates new
symbols and new understandings. The whole process involves an assimilation of
previously warded-off experience with a resultant change in the self.

It is important that the therapist listens out for key phrases or ways of
describing experiences or symptoms that may have personal meaning for the
client. The more deeply and personally an individual describes their experiences, the greater the likelihood they will use *personal meaning language*.
Language that not only describes their physical or emotional experience but
language that also contains symbolic imagery. Although many people may
meet the criteria for clinical depression, no two individuals who are suffering
from depression will describe their inner feeling state using the same language, providing they are encouraged to stay with and explore that feeling
state by the therapist's holding symbolic attitude.

The same is true for physical symptoms, such as physical pain. It is not that
the depression or the physical problem is not real. It is real and experienced
by the client. What we are seeking is the elaboration of the client's feeling
state and through this some access to their inner world. For a more detailed
account of this process, see Moorey and Guthrie (2003). In this paper, the
authors describe the therapy of a client seen by Robert Hobson for three sessions of treatment, termed two-plus-one therapy (Barkham and Hobson, 1989).

The client who is described in this paper has suffered from an extreme fear of thunderstorms for most of her life. Initially she uses *jam-jar language* to describe her fear and is disconnected from the fear itself. She actively avoids any reference to thunder and states that she wishes she was deaf and blind so she would never have to experience a thunderstorm again. As the session continues the client becomes more and more afraid as it begins to get dark outside. Hobson offers to move her chair so she does not have to face the window, which particularly unnerves her, as the sky is darkening and she fears a storm is approaching. She is appreciative of Hobson's offer to re-position the chairs and her anxiety falls.

As Hobson gently explores her symptoms using *understanding hypotheses*, and *focusing on her feelings*, there is a change in her language and she is able to talk in a different way. She describes a nightmare of being alone in her house and the house being struck by lightning. She talks about her anger with her daughter-in-law for leaving her children alone, and at her daughter-in-law's boyfriend for threatening to send the children away. As the session continues the fear of thunder begins to be understood as a symbol, not an absolute. It begins to undergo a process of symbolic transformation. The fear is large but it begins to be understood as a fear of something that is 'large and destructive' rather than only a fear of a thunderstorm itself.

The client recalls a memory from childhood of a time when her mother accused her of eating some 'best butter'. In the memory, the client denies it and becomes angry and swears at her mother. The memory is jumbled, but the sense from the memory is that the client felt she had done something really awful. In the retelling, the client remembers being sent to court and having to appear before a judge because she had sworn at her mother. Hobson doesn't try to make sense of the memory in a literal fashion but focuses upon the feelings and fears conveyed by the story. He stays with the client's immediate experience and uses the symbolic material to identify the underlying emotion; that she had done something 'dreadful', as if she had attacked her mother. Hobson then uses an *exploratory rationale* to link together her fear of thunder with previously warded-off fears about anger and destructiveness. There is an assimilation of these experiences and a change of self, with a subsequent reduction in her fear of thunderstorms.

Adopting a symbolic attitude means that the therapist must actively listen, recognise and take account of living symbols. This involves listening out for descriptions that convey personal meaning. Words like 'off balance' open up the possibility of movement and exploration as opposed to 'dizziness', which does not hold the same possibilities. To say 'I am depressed' conveys a generalised feeling state, but to say 'I feel as if a cloud has cast a dark shadow across my soul' conveys a deeply personal individual form of feeling, from which movement and exploration can occur.

The same process occurs with individuals' descriptions of physical symptoms. Many people may suffer from abdominal symptoms such as abdominal pain and distension plus an altered bowel habit and receive a diagnosis of irritable bowel syndrome. No two people with irritable bowel syndrome, however, will describe their experience in the same way, provided they are encouraged to describe their experience in depth, to a therapist who adopts a symbolic attitude.

Below are two brief descriptions of individuals describing their bowel symptoms in a therapeutic situation. Note how different the two descriptions are and the living symbols and turn of phrases that make each account unique.

Box 8.6 Example of a client describing her symptoms of irritable bowel syndrome (1)

CLIENT: It just comes away...I've no control over it...it's so smelly and disgusting...if I'm out, I'm so ashamed...I wait in the toilet until I think no one's in, and then I sneak out. I can't trust myself to be out.

In the example in Box 8.6, the client is conveying more than a description of her bowel symptoms, which are real and disabling. She is also conveying *personal meaning* by the choice of words she uses to describe her experience. She feels disconnected from herself and her gut is described as an 'it' over which she has no influence or power. She feels isolated and ashamed and uses two key phrases: 'I wait in the toilet until no one's in and then I sneak out' and 'I can't trust myself to be out'. The former implies a sense of living in shadows and the latter implies a fear perhaps of losing control. The exact meaning of these words is not important. In fact there isn't an exact meaning. What is important is that they open up an avenue of exploration that leads to the self and the possibility of a dialogue between the therapist and client which feels alive.

Box 8.7 An example of a client describing her symptoms of irritable bowel syndrome (2)

CLIENT: It starts with a sickly feeling...and then I know I'm in for trouble...all my insides begin to turn over...I have to rush upstairs...and then I'm in the loo for hours...no one else can get in...

As with the first example, the client in the example in Box 8.7 also views her bowel as separate from herself – a thing. However, apart from this, the description is entirely different. Key phrases include 'I know I'm in for trouble' and 'no one else can get in'. The former could imply many things but resonates with the image of a child realising he/she is going to be punished or told off. The latter is perhaps about keeping people away, shutting people out. The important thing is not to find any 'true' meaning, but that they open up opportunities to explore feeling states with the client and links to personal relationships.

Through symbolic transformation, conversations about both psychological and physical symptoms can lead to conversations about warded-off feelings with subsequent assimilation and change in the self.

Summary

In many respects the intermediate sessions are the most crucial in any brief therapy as there is a real chance to *build the relationship,* which is an essential feature of this model of treatment. There can be a tendency sometimes to coast in the intermediate sessions as a lot of the work involves returning again and again to similar themes and problems but slightly re-working them on each occasion. These building blocks of change are, however, crucial to the overall outcome and the therapist needs to be as attentive and proactive as in any other phase of the treatment. In the next chapter we will consider the final sessions, ending therapy and farewell letters.

9

The Final Sessions

Introduction

We usually consider the final phase of therapy, depending on the overall length of therapy, as comprising the last three or four sessions. In psychotherapy of any length not all the client's problems will be resolved by the end of therapy; the emphasis though in brief work is on starting a process that the client can continue after the therapy and contact with the therapist has ended. The seven key elements to consider are shown below and are outlined in the following sections:

1. Explicit discussion of ending
2. Link ending to previous loss or dilemmas regarding intimacy
3. Review the main problem
4. Review significant changes
5. Review how work can be continued by client
6. Farewell letter
7. Say goodbye

Towards the end of the chapter, we will also discuss the role of review sessions in the context of delivering brief psychotherapy and the potential changes that can occur after psychotherapy has been completed.

1. Explicit discussion of the ending

In brief therapy, it is often usual to refer to the ending of the therapy right from the beginning. This is obviously important in a three- or four-session therapy but even if the therapy is due to last for 16 sessions or longer, the therapist should provide the client with an expected ending time, right at the start of treatment. This does not have to be a specific date, but an approximate time. For example: 'So...we are going to meet for 16 sessions which will take us through until the middle of July.'

As the therapy reaches its final stage, which for a 16-session therapy will probably be the last four sessions, discussion of the ending should become explicit. Where there is a particular concern about endings, it can be flagged up several times during the therapy, but the last three to four sessions would be the minimum. Many patients develop deep attachments to their therapist, even if the therapy is short. Even if some clients do not outwardly show any concern, there is always the possibility that they may still have strong feelings, fears and concerns about the ending. Skill, compassion and understanding on behalf of the therapist are required to manage the ending successfully. It is useful to agree an actual finishing date a few sessions from the end of therapy. This automatically raises the spectre of ending and enables the therapist to explore the client's feelings about the ending.

2. Link ending to previous loss or dilemmas regarding intimacy

The ending of therapy often resonates with previous experiences of loss in the client's life. The therapist will probably already be aware of these losses and how the client has coped with loss in the past. Denial, anger, pain and distress are common ways we all can react to losing someone who is close to us. The whole approach of the model and specifically the Stage 2 competencies, which involve working in the *here and now*, using *I and we* and using *linking hypotheses*, provide a way of exploring and sharing with the client the difficulties of ending.

Box 9.1 Raising the ending

THERAPIST: Er...before we go on today...er I just need to say that we've got four sessions, including today, until the end of the therapy...er...I make that Monday the 16th of April...unless you are planning to be away before...or anything.

CLIENT: No...I'm not away.

(Continued)

(Continued)

THERAPIST: It's a bit hard to think about…ending…us not meeting… [*Understanding hypothesis*]

CLIENT: It's just gone so fast…I can't believe it's gone so fast…we barely seem to have started…

THERAPIST: Much…it is hard…and it sounds as if you feel…a bit short changed, I'm not sure. [*Understanding hypothesis*]

CLIENT: I just feel I can talk to you and it's going to be so hard to start again…I just get passed from pillar to post.

THERAPIST: [pauses and leans forward] you feel a bit like a parcel…

CLIENT: I've always been let down…I just expect it…it doesn't matter.

THERAPIST: Your feelings about this are important…you are feeling very let down.

CLIENT: It doesn't matter, why should it matter?

THERAPIST: Ah…well…you're are pulling away from me there…I think when we stop meeting…it does matter I think…it matters quite a bit to you. [*I and we*] …I wonder if you could stay with how you feel…now. [Therapists gestures with hand] [*Focus on feelings*]

CLIENT: No one cares…it's like no one cares…I feel I don't exist…

THERAPIST: Almost like there's nothing of you… [*Understanding hypothesis*]

CLIENT: Umh.

THERAPIST: and you're feeling…I don't care…and your mum didn't care. [*Linking hypothesis*]

CLIENT: It's like…how can I go on…it's just me…everything's so hard.

THERAPIST: Well…it's not easy…it's hard…to feel your own mum doesn't love you… You feel like giving up…it's not fair…

CLIENT: Why does it hurt so much…she's been dead for ten years?

THERAPIST: I wonder if you can stay with the hurt feeling…because in a way…I think if you can face that feeling or share some of it with me…there isn't such a need to keep it at bay… [*Focus on feelings*]

In the example in Box 9.1, the therapist raises the ending with the client and is aware of the resonances of the ending of therapy with the loss the client feels in relation to her own mother. The therapist tries to acknowledge the understandable distress from the client and uses the model competencies to try to stay with feelings.

3. Review the main problem

It is helpful to keep in mind the main problem or symptoms that the client originally sought help for, and it is to be hoped there will have been some improvement in this area. It is likely that this will have been continually discussed throughout the therapy but some overall review of the progress of the client's problem should be attempted. There may have been a gradual improvement, or ups and downs, or an improvement followed by a relapse as the therapy nears its conclusion.

It is important that the therapist presents a positive view of the future regarding the client's symptoms, with some acknowledgement that symptoms may return if the client experiences stress. Strategies or solutions which have been worked out in therapy should be reviewed and thought given to how the client may be enabled to react differently now.

As we have discussed before in several previous chapters, 'the problem' will be present in the final sessions, as it has been throughout the therapy, and it is important that the therapist attends to the 'here and now' as well to the overall bigger picture. In the example in Box 9.2 the client is talking about what she will be doing the week following the end of her 16-week therapy. She starts to talk about having her bathroom refurnished.

Box 9.2   Example of 'the problem' in a final session of therapy

CLIENT: I've got a lot planned for next week. I am having a new bathroom fitted, so I'll have the builders in all week…it's going to be chaos…

THERAPIST: Lots of mess. [Smiling]

CLIENT: Yes…but in a good way…I've got to pick the tiles…I haven't done that yet.

  [Client looks at the therapist and smiles…there is a feeling of warmth between them]

THERAPIST: Sounds like you are going to be busy…

CLIENT: Yes…and I'm sure they will over run…builders always do…they set to do one thing and then unearth some other problem that they then have to sort…it always takes longer and of course…it always costs more that you originally agree…[Client looks away…and there is a pause…the therapist picks up cue and notices a sense of discomfort in the client]

In the example in Box 9.2, the task for the therapist is not to be drawn into a lengthy discussion about bathrooms during the last session of therapy, but to try to understand what the client is trying to say to the therapist, and to maintain a symbolic attitude towards what is being discussed. We can only make informed guesses. We do not know what the client wants to say to the therapist, but it is likely to be something more than wanting to talk about bathrooms.

From the brief interaction shown in Box 9.2 we know that there is a shared feeling of warmth between the client and therapist. The client is talking about being busy and embarking on a project to 'rebuild' part of her home. This might be a way of saying to the therapist, 'Look...I am going to be ok...I am going to keep myself busy and I am going to continue the work of therapy by continuing to "rebuild" myself.' On the other hand, it could be a way of saying, 'look...it's going to be really hard to stop seeing you...the only way I will cope...is by keeping myself busy'. The client then goes on to talk about the builders 'unearthing problems' that were not immediately apparent at the outset of the work. Although it may seem fanciful, this next passage seems to imply a clear reference to the work of therapy, particularly because the client uses the word 'unearth'.

In the PI model, we are not seeking the 'real' meaning of what the client is saying, but to recognise that there is a deeper communication than that which appears to be happening in relation to the conversation about bathrooms. The problem is that the client cannot put the deeper communication into words, and that is 'the problem' that is in the room. As we have reiterated throughout the manual, the way a PI therapist would approach this problem would be to try to get in touch with the feeling that the client is experiencing (and the therapist may also be experiencing something of this as well) and to stay with the feeling, to see what emerges. In the example in Box 9.3, the conversation between client and therapist in Box 9.2 is continued.

Box 9.3   Focusing on feelings

CLIENT: Yes...and I'm sure they will overrun...builders always do...they set to do one thing and then unearth some other problem that they then have to sort...it always takes longer and of course...it always costs more that you originally agree...[client looks away...and there is a pause...the therapist notices a sense of discomfort in the client]

THERAPIST: [therapist leans forward towards client] I wonder if you could say a little about how you are feeling now. [Emphasises the word now]

CLIENT: Er...a bit cut off really...

THERAPIST: A bit distant from me...

CLIENT: I think there are lots of things I want to say...will want to say...when I walk out of here...but I can't think of them now.

THERAPIST: Those things may be important things...but you can't quite bring them to mind...it's frustrating when that happens...and I guess...it's one of the things that happens quite a lot with you...I wonder if we can just stay with how you are feeling and see if some words come to mind...

[Pause]

CLIENT: I think I am going to miss coming here...I mean...I'm still finding it hard to deal with things...

THERAPIST: Yes...of course...deal with things by yourself, without seeing me...helping...to some extent but difficult...still difficult.

CLIENT: Yes...I think it's helped...helped a lot...but...

THERAPIST: But...you feel let down...perhaps...

CLIENT: I feel that you've helped...and I'm grateful for that but...is that it...I've still got to cope with everything...and you know I think I can...

THERAPIST: I think you can too...but it's hard to stop meeting...and a big step to carry on with what we've been talking about...and I think you are feeling a bit let down by me?...

CLIENT: A bit...

THERAPIST: I come along and we talk about your problems, and share some very difficult things...and then...I walk off...so to speak...at least that's how it might feel...exploited even...i'm not sure...maybe that's a bit strong.

CLIENT: No...I think you mean well...I'm angry with myself...just angry it has to end...I wanted to thank you really...I haven't been able to say what I wanted to say...because...it's just naff really...but you have helped me...a lot...[makes eye contact with therapist and smiles]...I am a bit cross with you...[smiles]

In traditional psychodynamic therapy, the therapist may have offered an interpretation linking aspects of the client's story about the new bathroom suite and the transference relationship between the client and therapist. There are some obvious links, in particular the notion that the builders have come in, produced chaos and unearthed hidden problems. There is also the notion that the builders in some way may have exploited the client by charging more than what was originally agreed for the bathroom work to be carried out.

In PI therapy, however, the therapist will try to focus on the interactions and feelings between the client and therapist rather than the possible meaning of what is being talked about. The problem in the room is that the client has difficulty expressing her feelings towards the therapist. She has difficulty expressing both positive and negative feelings. She feels simultaneously warmth and attachment towards the therapist but also anger towards her that the therapy is ending. This micro problem is indicative of the problem area the therapist and client have been working on throughout the therapy, that the client finds it difficult to ask for help, finds it difficult to trust and feel close to people for fear of being rejected.

By staying with the client's experiencing in the 'here and now', the therapist is able to help the client express her feelings directly towards the therapist.

Instead of this leading to a negative outcome, there is a sense of the client being able to face her difficulties, resulting in a more positive connection with the therapist. The conversation continues in Box 9.4.

Box 9.4   Focusing on the problem

THERAPIST: [Picking up from Box 9.3] And you have every right to be cross with me...it's a very difficult thing to share things in the way you have... and it's a very difficult thing when that time for sharing comes to an end...but in a way...I think...you are more able to talk about how you feel and more able to manage difficulties...just like you have now...

CLIENT: Yes...I think I would have just put up with things. Not said anything. I do feel more in control of things and the bathroom is a positive thing for me. I've not done anything like this for a long time. I know I'm going to be busy...but it's a nice busy...rather than the frantic way I used to feel.

---

4. Review significant changes

In the last few sessions, the therapist should highlight and revisit significant changes that the client has made during the therapy. These will have been discussed previously but should be reviewed in the context of ending. They may well be included in the farewell letter (see later) and may be discussed in that context. The intention is to build upon changes that have occurred in the therapy so that these processes can continue when the therapy finishes, as shown in Box 9.5.

Box 9.5   Reviewing changes

THERAPIST: I think when we first met, you felt very down and trapped. You talked about not having any time for yourself and feeling put upon by others. It was very difficult for you to talk about how you felt. You keep a lot inside...and we talked about being a bit wary of people and afraid that if you opened up a bit...people wouldn't like you.

CLIENT: I think that's changed quite a lot actually. I feel much more sure of myself...and I don't really know...it kind of seems silly now...how I got into that state.

THERAPIST: Well it didn't seem silly to me...it's very hard to overcome things we fear...and you have worked very hard to do that...a fear of not being liked or not being likeable can become a BIG thing...it can become large...

CLIENT: I don't think it will ever go...

THERAPIST:	No...but I think...it doesn't feel as big...and just now...when you were talking about the end...I think you were able to say things to me that you would not have been able to do before...
CLIENT:	Oh...yeah...no...I wouldn't have said anything at all. I feel a lot more comfortable with people...and a lot less angry with my mum...I think seeing you has helped me understand her problems a lot more.

5. Review how work can be continued by the client

Our experience with this model is that continued change can occur and does occur after therapy has finished. The intention is that small changes can continue to occur post-therapy and may even result in bigger changes. If the client has begun to be more assertive in relationships and has recognised the benefits of this change, the therapist needs to emphasise the importance of maintaining this change. The same is true of a client who has become less defensive and is more trusting of people, and indeed true for any major change in interpersonal functioning.

Box 9.6 Maintaining changes

THERAPIST:	I think one of the things that really moved things forward was the dream you brought about being in an old house with a roof that was peppered with holes, and light was shinning threw those holes. The feeling in the dream was of intense unease and discomfort.
CLIENT:	That helped me put into words how I felt.
THERAPIST:	You used the word 'leaky'.
CLIENT:	Yes...like a leaky roof, I couldn't somehow keep people out, or stop them from hurting me...I couldn't keep myself in...I felt exposed.
THERAPIST:	And...you felt a bit of that here...
CLIENT:	Yes...yes...but I haven't had that dream...any more...
THERAPIST:	When we finish after today...you are going to be in situations, where some of those feelings...of being exposed...may come back...
CLIENT:	Yes...I know...but in a way...thinking about the dream helps me...I know that's what's happening and I somehow it doesn't feel as bad...I feel I can handle things differently...Yeah...I do feel that... and if I have a fit...I have a fit...so what...

(Continued)

(Continued)

THERAPIST: The fear of having a fit has been bigger than the actual fits...you have had...

CLIENT: Oh definitely...I was going to say...I had a fit last week...at football... in front of all the kids...right at the side of the football pitch. One of the parents apparently came over...she's a doctor...and I was looked after and taken to hospital...but it just hasn't been a problem... For me...I was back in school two days later...and it's been fine...

THERAPIST: That's amazing...

CLIENT: Yes...In the past...I would have been mortified...I wouldn't have been able to go back into school...to have a fit...right in the middle of football, with all the school watching...I would have died... it would have been my worst nightmare...but it's happened and it was ok...

There are often significant events in people's lives that are going to occur after the therapy, which may benefit from discussion prior to ending, especially if the client has made positive changes during the treatment. For example, it may be helpful to go through with the client how he/she will cope with a key anniversary, or a family wedding, or similar event that resonates with the client's past difficulties and to contrast the new ways of coping with the client's past ways of behaving. An example of this is given in Box 9.7

Box 9.7   Anticipating future difficult events

THERAPIST: I know after we finish today...You are going to be facing Kika's birthday next month...it's the 9th...isn't it...

CLIENT: Yes...I'm dreading it...but my sister is coming over and we are going to get a lot of balloons and blow them up and take them to her grave. My sister's then going to stay over and we'll probably have a takeaway and a bottle of wine, after we've put the kids to bed.

THERAPIST: It's a very difficult day for you...

CLIENT: I just have to get through it...but rather than hide away by myself... which is what I've done...the last 2 years...I'm going to have my sister there...I think that's a better thing to do. Plus I won't drink myself into oblivion like I did before...

THERAPIST: That's been a really big thing you've done...to cut down how much you drink...it's taken a lot of strength and will power to do that...

> CLIENT: I think I just got to a point, where I realised that I was just getting through the nights...by drinking...not in front of the boys...after I had put them to bed...but I think it's affected them...because since I've stopped doing that...they seem so much better...all the shouting I used to do has stopped and I just thought the other day...I actually really enjoy being with them...
>
> THERAPIST: That's a quite a special moment for you.

6. Farewell letter

Written communications between client and therapist are common in psychotherapy but relatively rare in psychodynamic and relational therapies. They have been developed most explicitly in cognitive analytic therapy (CAT; Ryle and Kerr, 2002).

Farewell letters in PI therapy were first used in 1996 in the context of a randomised trial which was set up to evaluate the cost-effectiveness of PI therapy versus an anti-depressant versus usual care in patients with severe and intractable irritable bowel syndrome (Creed et al., 2003). The rationale for using farewell letters was based on four assumptions. First, letters appeared to be of clinical value in CAT (another form of relational therapy). Second, the patients who were taking part in the trial were being asked to complete a variety of formal measures of assessment, including diaries of symptoms and symptom questionnaires, so the work was more active than traditional psychodynamic models. Third, a key part of the therapeutic process was the exploration of the patient's physical symptoms, with a view to discovering connections with important emotional and interpersonal issues. It was hypothesised that a letter at the end of therapy may help to reinforce these associations. Finally, the therapy was brief, and it was thought the letter might facilitate continuation with the work of therapy after it had finished and also help with the actual ending of therapy itself.

A one-year evaluation of the letters was carried out, which involved sending out a questionnaire to clients who had completed therapy (Howlett and Guthrie, 2001). All reported that they had kept the letter and most had read it several times during the year post-therapy. Several people reported sharing the letter with key people in their lives including partners, grown-up children and close friends. The letter appeared to help people share their experiences with others and increased possibilities of confiding. Clients reported consulting the letter at times of difficulty and using it to aid problem-solving. Clients spoke of the value of the letter in very positive terms, and there was clear evidence that the letter had facilitated the work of therapy after the sessions had ended (Howlett and Guthrie, 2001).

For a small number of clients who had not found therapy helpful, the letter did not convey any additional value and one client reported that it had a deleterious effect as it brought up memories she found distressing. In view of this we recommend that letters are given to clients who are reporting benefits from the therapy, but may be best left out if there has been little improvement, unless there is a particular indication.

We suggest the therapist should introduce the idea of the letter during the initial sessions of therapy. An example of how this might be done is given in Box 9.8. The nature and purpose of the letter should be discussed and agreed. The letter has been incorporated into the model and used in all forms of brief therapy, even therapy as short as four sessions (Guthrie et al., 2001).

Box 9.8 Example: introduction of letter

THERAPIST: As we've met now on a couple of occasions I'd like to discuss with you a letter that I write towards the end of therapy which will summarise the things we have talked about over the course of our meetings. We've found it's helpful for people to take this letter away with them when the therapy is over...er we have another ten sessions after today...as it helps people remember the things we've talked about.

CLIENT: Ok.

THERAPIST: The letter is just for you and will not be sent to your GP or anyone else...I usually include significant things we've discussed...which I think may be helpful to keep in mind...I will discuss with you the kinds of things that may be useful to put in the letter...and I will show you a draft version which you can amend or change...before we agree the final version...I will also write a more formal brief letter to your GP about the outcome of the therapy...er...It's good practice to do this... but I won't include any personal details in that letter...and you will also receive a draft copy of this much shorter GP letter...before it is sent so you can provide me with any comments etc.

CLIENT: So I get two letters?

THERAPIST: Yes...a long and personal one from me to you...and a copy of a brief letter I will write to your GP...I should say at this point that if we decide through discussions that you don't wish to receive a letter from me...or you don't think it will be helpful etc....then I won't write one...so any summary will be done through discussions between you and me.

CLIENT: No...it sounds like a good idea.

The farewell letters are demanding and time-consuming to write. The therapist should write the letter as the therapy progresses and not wait until the end to try to do this. It is helpful if the therapist jots down notes when listening to the audio recording after each session and where possible uses the client's own language to bring life to the words. The therapist should imagine what the client may feel like when he/she reads the letter, and it should be couched in such a way that the client will experience the letter in a positive way.

There should be a narrative that follows from the first session and tracks the client's progress during therapy. The letter should explicitly address the ending of therapy with suggestions of how the work can continue even when the therapy has actually stopped. There should be no surprises in the letter and everything should be familiar to the client.

Each letter will be different and may vary slightly in the structure and content. What is important is to capture meaningful shared moments in the therapy with which the client can re-connect, if they read it again some months later. Box 9.9 summarises key things to include in the letter, but it is not an exhaustive list and not all of these things need to be included in every letter. The therapist will need to use judgement and discuss the content of the letter in supervision.

Box 9.9   Content of the letter

- A description of the problem, with which the client presented during the initial session, using the client's own words.
- Moments of shared feeling, living symbols and metaphor, which should include how these were explored.
- An exploratory rationale which links symptoms, feelings and relationships, including where relevant a model.
- Problematic patterns in relationships and how these have impacted on the client.
- Avoided, painful or warded-off feelings.
- Progress in therapy including reduction in warded-off feelings, closer sharing of problems with therapist and changes in relationships outside therapy.
- A timeline which refers to change over the course of therapy.
- A timeline which refers to past, present and future.
- Acknowledgement of the ending.
- Reference to the changes that can be continued post-therapy.

A draft version of the farewell letter should be produced and discussed with the client during the penultimate session of therapy, although as discussed above, the therapist should be continually adding to it and changing it over the course of the therapy. In the final session, the therapist can start the session by reading out the amended version of the letter, or read the letter out when it seems appropriate. It's important, however, not to leave it until the end of the session. It is important that the client has ownership of the letter and its content, and the above process usually results in very positive and favourable feedback. An example of a farewell letter is shown in Box 9.10.

Box 9.10   Example of a farewell letter

Dear John

This is a letter from me to you, and it will not be sent to your GP or any other health professional. I would like to say from the outset how much I have enjoyed meeting you and sharing time with you. This letter is intended as brief summary and reminder of the things we have discussed over the last few weeks.

I remember that you were rather puzzled at being referred to see me, and were understandably hesitant and rather unsure when we first met. You had seen your GP on several occasions in the last year for a variety of problems including feeling tired and exhausted, pains in your tummy, headaches, feeling sick, not being able to sleep and feeling down all the time. You told me that your GP felt you were stressed and although you agreed with that you could not see how talking about 'it' would help.

When I asked you what you most wanted help with, you said you just wanted it all to stop. You felt you couldn't settle, you couldn't relax, and when we stayed with that feeling, you told me you wanted 'the pain' to stop. You told me the pain felt like there was a big wound inside you, a wound that couldn't heal. You felt it constantly and were never free of this awful feeling from the time you woke up in the morning to when you fell asleep at night, usually having had to drink a bottle of wine to 'knock yourself out'.

You are a private person. You are someone who prefers to keep their thoughts and feelings to themselves, so it was a new experience for you to share something of how you were feeling with me. I remember you telling me that it would be impossible to talk to your family about your feelings as you were the person that they relied on to be strong, and indeed you are a strong person and took responsibility from an early age for your little brother after you were both taken into care and later adopted.

As we talked more, you were able to share some of the dreadful nightmares you were experiencing and had experienced for many years. At first, you wanted to know from me what these dreams meant as if there would be one explanation. Instead, we found they were a way of exploring and sharing some of the fears and feelings you had kept hidden inside for many years. You told me about the feelings of panic you felt inwardly if ever you were asked to do something or face something. You always faced it of course, and no one else would know except you how dreadful you felt inside.

The more we talked, the more there seemed to be connections and parallels between things that had happened in your life. Having to be strong for your wife when so many awful things had happened to her seemed very like having to be strong for your little brother.

The more you love someone, the more at times you can feel frustrated with them, and angry with them, especially if they let you down in some way. In the last couple of sessions, you have shared some of these difficult feelings too. You do get angry at times and resentful and annoyed and 'pissed off' with people. You feel they always expect you to cope and be cheerful and just breeze through life, yet until recently that is how you behave. We have wondered together, how could they know that you get upset and angry and fed up, when you never tell them or let them know. It's almost as if you've expected them to know, to know how you are feeling inside, even though you never show it.

We have also touched on deeper feelings and fears. Your fear of death which is very great and also your fear that others close to you will die, and even the fear that in some way you may be responsible. I have admired how resilient and 'strong' you have been and how even when suffering yourself, you did care and have always cared for others.

As we are reaching the final session, it feels like a lot has changed. You have felt physically a lot better over the last few weeks. You are more active, and feel more refreshed. The dreams have stopped and you are actually contemplating returning to work on a part-time basis. We have puzzled how your physical health can be connected to your emotional world. It's not clear and it certainly isn't straightforward. Your gut symptoms started with an infection, so this would have triggered an inflammatory response in the bowel. It really threw you physically and emotionally as for the first time in your life you could not be strong when you felt you were needed. My feeling is that this threw you into a state of panic, and some of the feelings you had buried for many years began to emerge, if only in your dreams at first. The body and mind are not separate and the more physically unwell you became the more 'stressed' emotionally until a vicious circle developed. You couldn't sleep, you felt exhausted, the physical and mental pain was unbearable, your resilience was finally shattered.

It's very hard to think that we will be meeting for the last time. Although we have talked about ending during the therapy, it still can seem like a shock when it finally happens. Because you have suffered such traumatic losses, any loss no matter how small is significant. As we have discovered, loss for you is mixed up with a lot of different feelings including panicky fears, distress, anger and upset and deep pain. Most of all, it feels like a wound. A wound that has never healed and for most of your life you have kept hidden.

I think you have made some big changes in the last few weeks and I hope that you can continue to work on these in the next few months. As we have discovered it's not actually what you share and talk about that is always the most important thing, it's the feeling that you get from being able to share things. May I take this opportunity to wish you and your family all the very best.

7. Say goodbye

It may seem obvious but it is very important to say goodbye to a client and, just as a lot can happen in the first few moments of therapy, a lot can happen in the last few moments. Saying goodbye is difficult for many people, including therapists, which is why we have highlighted the importance of this basic human transaction.

Brief therapy is about taking something of value forward. The significance of warm words from the therapist at the end of treatment, including a warm handshake, whilst looking the client in the eye, should not be forgotten.

Review sessions

The structure of some therapies includes a review session which takes place 6–12 weeks after the therapy has been completed. We have used this format with very brief therapies for self-harm (four sessions) and found that an additional session a few weeks later helps to solidify gains from the therapy and contain risk. Follow-up sessions are fairly common in many brief therapies and they provide clients with an opportunity to come back and review their progress after the end of therapy. Clients are often able to gain a greater perspective of how the therapy has helped them and how they are putting into practice the changes or things they have learnt from the therapy sessions.

Follow-up sessions can also act as an emotional life-line for clients who have found ending difficult. The letter also helps with this aspect of ending and the therapist and client will also use the time in the follow-up session to reflect on the letter and how the client has used it. They may discuss that the client has shown the letter to other important people in their lives and their reactions to this.

Summary

The last three chapters have provided an overview of the therapy in practice. In combination with Chapters 4 to 6, they convey, as best as any psychotherapy manual is able to, the general approach of PI therapy when used in a brief format. In some of the studies on the model we have changed the length of the first session so that it can last for up to two to three hours. We have found this of benefit for clients who suffer from persistent physical symptoms or who are difficult to engage. The fundamental approach of the model, however, is similar no matter what the presenting problem and, for the purposes of this book, we have preferred to include a generic manual that can be used for clients with a wide range of presenting problems or conditions.

PART III

LEARNING AND DEVELOPING THE MODEL

10

Being an Effective Practitioner of Psychodynamic-Interpersonal Therapy: Developing Competence

This chapter introduces some of the key elements that arise when helping therapists to become effective practitioners of PI therapy. Therapists can adhere to a manual of therapy but not be remotely competent and this chapter goes beyond adherence to look at how competence and expertise can be developed. We are concerned with helping therapists to become as competent and skilful as they can be, and to be able to maintain those skills in the long term.

Unlike others who have developed schools of psychotherapy, Bob Hobson was keen that the PI therapy maintained a principle that it can be used by a non-specialist in psychotherapy such as a nurse working in physical medicine or a psychiatrist working in a secure unit just as much as a psychologist working full-time as a psychotherapist. This does not mean that therapy cannot be differentiated into different levels of expertise, but we have followed Hobson's principle that these are not organised as a hierarchy of importance.

Undoubtedly, some therapists are notable for having exceptionally good outcomes. Others may be especially resilient in managing clients who challenge boundaries and make great demands on the therapist. It follows from this breadth that the mark of a good, safe PI therapist lies in knowing one's strengths and weaknesses. This chapter does not define a training programme to lead to a specific qualification, but it does provide an overview and some suggestions for developing expertise for individuals and groups of professionals.

As discussed in the manual section of the book, Hobson draws a useful analogy here with playing 'scales' and improvisation (Hobson, 1985: 207).

A skilled musician can improvise based on a particular scale that has been practised previously. Each performance is different but the underlying structure is
shaped by the detailed knowledge of that particular scale. By analogy, a psychotherapist can become skilled in using a scale but does not need to be consciously
aware every second as the material is so familiar and well practised:

> The procedures are akin to the scales of notes for a musician or to the words and
> phrases of a literary artist. Broad theoretical ideas and psychodynamic formulations
> are of importance only in so far as they are incarnated in the minute particulars of
> what we do. We need to practise our scales. Technical accomplishment is essential
> in achieving a unique 'true' voice of feeling. (Hobson, 1985: 207)

Before offering suggestions about developing expertise in this particular model
of therapy, we have briefly reviewed some key points about expertise in psychotherapy more generally.

Adherence and competence

Adherence refers to the extent to which a therapist conducts a therapy as it is
described and defined in a manual (Waltz et al., 1993). These elements are
crucial in defining and differentiating an intervention in a research study but
may be less well suited to developing clinical skills in practice. The adherence
scale for PI therapy was originally developed in a research context (Startup and
Shapiro, 1993). It covers elements that differentiate this model from others, but
also includes some 'facilitating conditions' that are relevant to all therapists.
The scale has been modified so that the elements reflect closely the skills we
have discussed within the manual (Chapters 4 to 6) and only includes PI therapy items. The modified version of the scale is available in Appendix 1 so that
therapists can monitor their level of skill development using audio recordings.

In contrast, *competence* is 'the extent to which the therapists conducting the
interventions take the relevant aspects of the therapeutic context into account and
respond to those contextual variables appropriately' (Waltz et al., 1993). Competence,
therefore, involves skills like timing of interventions; how to choose which possible
intervention; when to hold back; and also subtler skills related to the precise form
of language used in a conversation. These aspects are much more difficult to rate
reliably but are often the focus of clinical training as discussed later.

Learning PI therapy

Before the model was even described, Robert Hobson had already pioneered the
use of audio and video recording feedback for teaching and supervision. He
established the routine use of recordings in supervision and he was one of the
pioneers in the use of video recordings as a teaching medium to model how
therapists work. From the outset, learning from feedback was intrinsic to this
way of working. Hobson developed a repertoire of ways of introducing new

therapists to effective practice, and his systematic use of feedback from sessions is still as relevant today.

The process of developing PI therapy in a research context is fully described in the original reports (Goldberg et al., 1984; Maguire et al., 1984), but the research is relevant here primarily in terms of the development of teaching methods. The research team had been influenced by the work of Ivey et al. (1968) in the use of micro-skills teaching of counselling and therapy, but in this context it applied for the first time to a relational form of therapy. The micro-skills method involves the definition, modelling and practice of desirable therapeutic behaviours until there is mastery of each component. This was in part accomplished through three teaching recordings introducing basic skills, putting the skills into practice and rehearsing the key skills.

In summary the early phase of development of the model in terms of teaching showed:

- The model can be described clearly and rated with a measure that is reliable (Goldberg et al., 1984).
- A simple micro-skills teaching package using inexperienced teachers had a dramatic effect on changing trainees behaviour from an interrogatory style to a negotiated style (Maguire et al., 1984).
- Supplementary group teaching increased the trainees' level of confidence (Moss et al., 1991).
- After two years there had been little if any change in the trainees' ability to use these skills (Moss et al., 1991).
- The original teaching material (derived from actual therapies in a pilot phase) was re-made with simulated interviews of high plausibility (Margison and Moss, 1994).
- The method has subsequently been used widely and replicated with nurse trainees (Paxton et al., 1988).
- A factor analytic study of the pattern of skills acquired was consistent with the underlying model (Moss et al., 1991).

The research focused on the early stage of skills acquisition. To develop the model beyond the initial training or research contexts, further work was carried out using supplementary teaching methods to prepare practitioners for the range and complexity of problems found in everyday use as described below.

A further study (Guthrie et al., 2004b) showed that counsellors working in primary care could be trained efficiently to deliver PI therapy using this approach. As described in Chapter 3, 20 counsellors received a 12-week training course in PI therapy including supervised practice of cases from their primary care settings. The client outcomes were good, with 50% showing clinically significant and reliable change.

Performance was assessed using video recordings of sessions with simulated patients at three points in time: before training, after an intensive first week of training and at the end of 12 weeks of supervision. Counsellors' adherence to the model was assessed in relation to three patient scenarios: chronic depression, somatisation and suicidality. Validity of the simulated sessions was verified by reference to counsellor behaviour with actual patients using audio-recorded sessions. After training, counsellors' adherence to PI therapy increased without affecting their basic counselling skills. Counsellors working with patients with chronic depression or somatisation demonstrated improvement in specific items; there was, however, less evidence of model application among suicidal patients, where concerns about managing risk were predominant. Ratings of audio recordings of sessions with actual patients confirmed that counsellors were able to apply the model in a real-life situation. The counsellors also reported a positive experience with enhanced skills after training.

These teaching methods were also used in evaluating training in psychotherapy for social workers addressing PI behaviours among 14 core psychotherapeutic competences. This research showed the course to be effective overall (Firth et al., 1999). The training methods for both short courses for psychiatrists, nurses, counsellors, psychiatric social workers and clinical psychologists (e.g. Margison and Moss, 1994; Moss et al., 1991; Paley et al., 2003a, 2003b; Paxton et al., 1988) and as part of longer training (Firth et al., 1993) appear to be effective across professional groups.

Development of additional training methods: role-play

Role-plays are another way of hearing feedback about performance as a therapist. They have been used widely in developing therapist skills and awareness for this model of psychotherapy and as an adjunct to supervision of clinical experience. However, trainees are often worried that they will not be able to cope with 'difficult' situations that occur outside the immediate training context. So, from an early stage we drew on the work of Kagan (1980) to develop a way of addressing these therapist fears.

Kagan suggests that therapists typically 'feign clinical naiveté' with a supervisor to avoid possible humiliation about their basic fears. He described these as fear of being engulfed or engulfing (seducing) the other; or being attacked/ attacking the other. These are seen as the basic fears in any interpersonal interaction, but they are amplified in the close observation characteristic in learning psychotherapy. We used role-plays to set up a series of escalating difficulties to desensitise the trainees to their fears and to help them to discuss the difficulties they experienced in an open way. We developed four stages of increasing complexity and challenge for the trainee therapists.

In our adaptation of Kagan's methods, a standard format is used for all the role-plays (Margison, 1991). A group, typically of about four therapists in training and a facilitator, meet regularly. Two chairs are kept for the members currently playing therapist and client. The 'client' is asked to prepare a couple of sentences summarising the basic information about age, gender and main problems. Sometimes the role-play will be based on an initial session but role-players are also surprisingly adept at starting as though several sessions into an ongoing therapy. Either the client or the therapist (or occasionally both) are given cue cards which have a brief instruction explaining what should be done. Typically this is a brief statement about what is the 'agenda', such as assuming that the client has to be told that the therapist is going to be away for three weeks' holiday. The teacher stops the role-play after two or three minutes in the early examples, or somewhat longer in the later, more complex examples. After the role-play a standard sequence is followed with the two role-players expressing their feelings about the interaction before opening up the discussion to the whole group. It is crucial in this teaching method to establish an atmosphere that is conducive to learning. Other group members are encouraged to describe what they saw, heard or felt. Also they are asked to comment about how they might have felt as the client or responded as the therapist. Criticism of the 'therapist' is specifically discouraged. See Table 10.1 for examples of role-play cards.

Commonly trainees have had bad previous experiences of role-plays where they have felt humiliated or exposed. So, it is important for the teacher to establish an atmosphere that allows exploration in depth for the role-players within a safe framework. In a group that has been working together for only a few weeks it is usually possible for the members to be quite open about their anxieties as therapists. A reliable structure of the teaching session prevents inappropriate drift towards the training group becoming a quasi-therapeutic group.

Table 10.1 Examples of role-play cards

Role-Plays Level One: Examples

- Avoid all eye contact with your client/therapist
- Speak only technical jargon
- Ask only direct factual questions

Role-Plays Level Two: Examples

- You are taking an unplanned three-week holiday after the next session
- Discuss your need to change the session time

Role-Plays Level Three: Examples

- Do not accept what your client/therapist says at face value
- Comment in an emotionally neutral tone about some aspect of your client/therapist's appearance or clothing

Role-Plays Level Four: Examples

- Discuss with your therapist that you fear you might lose control and smash things/harm yourself
- Discuss feeling embarrassed but that you need to tell your therapist how attracted you are to him/her
- Tell your therapist that his/her habit of pausing before answering is driving you crazy

The training begins with low key examples of how sensitive the therapeutic situation is to therapist behaviour. So, for example, a trainee may be given a prompt card, which instructs the therapist to be 'over-reassuring', 'lean too close to the patient', 'avoid eye contact' or similar undesirable behaviours. The therapist can use these early examples to become sensitive to nuances in the interpersonal situation and also become less anxious about the role-play itself. This is preparation for the next phase when the sessions focus on how to make practical arrangements about breaks, reviews of progress, session times. These particular role-plays have a dual purpose: the experience allows the therapist to be able to structure a therapy with confidence whilst developing sensitivity to the undercurrents of the therapy.

A common error amongst beginners is their tendency to equate listening with passivity and as a result they may give insufficient structure. Whilst learning these basic techniques of structure and contracts they also become more sensitive to the emotional undercurrents involved in negotiating apparently practical issues. For example, any issue related to timing or frequency may be linked with separation issues or feeling neglected. Issues regarding review of progress are often tinged with feelings of being criticised or, in extreme cases, humiliation and narcissistic wounds. This second phase of the role-play training prepares the therapist for the inevitable multiple levels involved in any therapeutic conversation.

The third group of role-plays focuses on how easily the therapeutic alliance can be damaged and persecutory dynamics established. For example, one role-play simply asks *both* participants not to take anything the other says at face value. As this is enacted the trainee becomes aware of the risk of invalidating the other's experience. This helps the trainee to understand the processes described by Meares and Hobson (1977) as a 'persecutory spiral'. By enacting the patient role as well it is possible for the trainee to realise just how sensitive the person in that position will be to minor discrepancies, ambiguities or inconsistencies in the therapist. These examples also give practice in how to repair ruptures in the therapeutic alliance.

Many beginning therapists in service contexts have had no experience of their own personal therapy, which is a prerequisite for most trainees wishing to practise primarily in psychotherapy. Whilst role-plays are clearly not capable of providing an equivalent experience, they can increase the trainee therapist's sensitivity to interpersonal nuances which otherwise are learned only through therapeutic failures with actual clients.

In the fourth stage of the role-play training, a series of role-plays deliberately simulates what Kagan described as 'therapeutic nightmares' such as being told of intense suicidal or violent impulses, sexual feelings towards the therapist and antagonistic and hurtful comments about the therapist. Kagan had developed a number of 'stimulus vignettes' on video recordings, which the trainee could watch and reflect on their emotional response. Our method draws on that technique, but uses a role-play situation to enact the challenging experience. The therapists have to think on their feet and respond in 'real time', but in a safe environment with no risk to clients. Most trainees find these sessions a demanding but positive experience.

After the formalised sequence of role-play situations it is possible to extend this model of training into actual clinical work. For example, in a supervision group a trainee can role-play his or her client, or can ask another group member to role-play the client whilst the trainee stays in the therapist role. The advantage of this method is that it allows the therapist to become familiar with 'What if?' scenarios in dealing with particularly challenging material.

We evaluated the effectiveness of this role-play training in acquiring therapy skills (Palmieri et al., 2007) and the findings suggested that role-play training was effective in learning new skills. A 15-item role-play competence measure was developed. Ratings by three judges of 34 role-plays from PI therapy training showed good inter-rater and internal reliability. Validity was supported as scores were statistically significantly associated with the length of psychotherapy training experience. Most participants achieved satisfactory ratings on the key skills of this model of therapy after the training.

These methods can be supplemented by the use of *peer teaching groups* first described by Kagan (1980) when the members rotate roles between the roles of commentator/time-keeper, facilitator, 'patient' and 'therapist'. These techniques are a particularly powerful way of getting across the idea of different therapeutic perspectives. When teaching resources are scarce it is possible to have several groups of more experienced trainees running simultaneously with teachers moving between the groups to add an additional perspective.

We have used these sessions regularly with therapists at different levels of experience and it is possible to develop new role-plays relevant to any specific topic such as working with somatic distress or managing self-destructive behaviour depending on the experience and clinical setting of the participants. Participants include established PI therapists who take part in the sessions to maintain their skills as part of continuing professional development.

With established therapists who want to progress to the role of supervisor we have used the same structure to role-play the difficulties that arise in a supervisory setting where members role-play supervisor and therapist and reflect on experiences with different styles of supervision.

Learning to study by observing sessions

A wide range of process methods has been developed to analyse what is happening within a therapeutic session and many have been used with PI therapy (see Chapter 3). In developing training for PI therapy we thought that it would be valuable to develop these methods derived from research in a teaching context. There is an almost infinite variety of ways in which such methods could be developed and the examples given below are to be seen as examples rather than definitive (see also Margison, 1991, 1999).

The first phase of this training encourages the trainee to listen closely to a session by transcribing part of the session as accurately as possible annotating the length of pauses, sections where both participants talk together, hesitations, non-verbal vocalisations, dysfluencies and changes in intonation. This is a time-intensive process, but it reminds the therapist of the complexity of what is happening across many channels of communication in a session. There are several systems in use for transcribing, and outside of the research setting it is not critical that validated methods are used to write down the interchange between therapist and client. However, it is a valuable skill to learn and we recommend, where possible, using a standardised system such as the one described by Mergenthaler and Stinson (1992).

After learning how to transcribe the session the trainee starts to write down process comments. The exact order in which these are introduced is not critical, but a suggested sequence is given which follows a logical development of skills (Margison, 1999) and this is reflected in the comments below.

What the therapist does

The therapist uses a method of describing the structure of *what* is said. Trainee therapists can use the rating manual in Appendix 1 to assess their own interventions. There is also a variety of alternative models discussed by Elliott and colleagues (1987) that can help a therapist see different ways of conceptualising a session.

Describing the intention behind each intervention

It is useful to distinguish *form* from *intent* in analysing therapeutic interventions. One option is to use a system that provides an accessible set of categories to distinguish different reasons why a particular intervention might be used, for example the List of Therapist Intentions (Hill and O'Grady, 1985). Discussion of the intentions behind interventions can feel very uncomfortable, but is helpful in developing self-reflective skills. They described some intentions focused on the therapist focusing on feelings, new knowledge and insight, whilst others concerned encouraging and maintaining change and setting limits. These provide little challenge to the therapist other than mastering new concepts. However, the final group focused on meeting the *therapist's* needs (whether to be liked, admired, respected or reassured) and these are much more challenging for therapists to acknowledge. It requires considerable trust to openly examine less honourable motives that may be driving some interventions. Robert Hobson encouraged this degree of honesty from those working with him but was always willing to share the experience by talking about difficulties he encountered as a therapist (see, for example, Hobson, 1985: 261–81).

How the client responds

From the early development of the model by Hobson it has been clear that mere acquiescence with the therapist's point of view is insufficient and that a fundamental test of an intervention is how far the client develops and extends imagery and feelings in their subsequent narrative. In developing this therapeutic skill the focus of the observation is what the client says in response to what the therapist says rather than the nature of the intervention.

Metaphor and therapy

Metaphor is an important concept in PI therapy and Hobson wrote extensively on this topic (for example Hobson, 1985: 55–61). Sometimes a therapist may use a metaphor or simile to illuminate a key point, but in this context we are more interested in amplifying and giving back the metaphors that arise in the client's everyday language. However, it is easy to miss the significance of an extended metaphor within a therapy and we need to develop our expertise in listening for examples that develop a shared feeling language. Sometimes these metaphors become important reference points that the therapist or client can refer to as a form of shorthand for an important shared experience.

One strategy for learning how to listen at this level is to attend specifically to every possible metaphor, even those which appear to have been used as part of customary vernacular speech (a cliché or dead metaphor). By simply listing such phrases from the transcript it is possible to draw up hypotheses about hidden material. (For a fuller discussion of this technique see Margison, 1995.) These words and phrases may be differentiated by being expressed with more energy or affect, but sometimes the therapist just needs to be aware of words like 'burden' or 'wasting' that can be picked up and amplified to develop hypotheses about core feelings, or words such as 'stuck' or 'wasted' to identify themes that may be related to blocked progress in the therapy. Metaphor (like the word transference) literally means to carry across. Metaphors in therapy carry meanings from one context to another.

Case formulation

There are definite advantages to using a formulation: Having a formulation shared with the patient can help maintain the therapeutic alliance during diffi-cult re-enactments; or, in supervision, help understand potential re-enactments. Also, the therapist can use the formulation after each session to ensure that the agreed focus is being maintained (Margison et al., 2000). At the session level, it is possible to link different sequences within the therapy to different elements of the case formulation and to use the formulation to maintain focus (see Margison, 1999).

There is an inevitable tension between different types of formulation. In this approach a formulation that is shared and developed within the conversa-tion is central. However, the therapist's role is sometimes to help map out the terrain by drawing on prior concepts and experience. Hobson was very aware of this tension when he wrote 'the form of a developing conversation often *is* the diagnosis and also the treatment' (Hobson, 1985: 177). He clarifies this seeming paradox when referring to a case example, that:

> In the interview we can formulate problems at different 'levels': in terms of the minute particulars of non-verbal behaviour, the disturbances of his central relation-ships and his struggle for identity in an adult world. A central and often difficult task in psychotherapy is to decide which problems are to be tackled at what 'levels'.
> (Hobson, 1985: 178)

This choice can be determined by many factors such as the time available for the therapy.

Modern approaches to psychotherapy are often 'formulation-driven' with a description of the problems; psychological explanations based on theory about the development and maintenance of these problems; a plan for intervention based on the theory and principles used; and predictions about how the therapeutic relationship will unfold (see for example, Johnstone et al., 2011).

PI therapy can be guided by this more formal approach to formulation, and can draw on psychodynamic and relational theory freely. However, the therapist needs to be aware of the potential to inadvertently depend upon 'jam-jar' thinking and block the collaborative aspects of the therapy by being too distracted by a formulation based on theory: it is always tempting to seek evidence to support a pre-existing theory.

A formulation can also be expressed in letter form as described in Chapter 9 and the letter can be a summary of the evidence discovered in the conversation between client and therapist. A written formulation is a distillation of what happens in the therapy, but it is best to see formulating as an ongoing process, based upon the minutiae of the 'here and now', always open to correction. So in the first five minutes the therapist needs to be especially sensitive to cues that may only become clear later in the session. The approach we recommend combines the formulation with the evidence supporting it. So, as Hobson suggests, we are trying to summarise the 'developing conversation' in ways that help to progress the therapy in a mutual and collaborative way.

The therapist is focusing upon 'the problem' that is alive in the session, and gathering information about patterns in past relationships and those in the present, both outside and inside therapy (described as the triangles of person and of conflict by Malan, 1979: 80). In each of these areas there may be explicit problems or concerns, and the client may have already seen patterns between them. The therapist is listening for key metaphors, phrases or symbols to summarise these patterns in the words of the client, and is also looking out for the 'minute particulars' – glances away, a catch in the voice – that may illuminate what is happening for the client, and the therapist is also being alert for internal clues such as bodily feelings – tension, nausea, tiredness, dry mouth – to give a further perspective on the conversation.

When writing up the notes after the session it is worth spending time on 'the first five minutes' rather than rushing to record the middle section of the session, as the early feelings and impressions may reveal an unexpected perspective. From the information gathered, therapists can write down their hypotheses about what is happening for the client, the therapist and their interaction. There may be links between different relationships or themes in the session (or to past sessions) and eventually the core of the formulation can be expressed in the form of an explanatory hypothesis (see Chapter 9). This process is much easier if there is a recording of the session, but it is worth putting down initial impressions quickly first in what are often referred to as 'process notes'.

Process notes

In this model of therapy process notes are closely linked with formulation building as described above. Initially therapists may simply attempt to transcribe what was said with no attempt to make sense of the material within a broader framework. It is helpful, as described in the section on formulation, to guide the trainee towards writing down what was actually said but then separately to generate hypotheses based on what the client said, what the therapist said and their interaction. At the end of the process notes the trainee can keep track of the overall therapy by commenting about progress linked with *core problems* and reminders for the next session such as themes to be monitored and predictions of what may happen in the next session. Table 10.2 shows a possible structure for recording process notes to assist in formulating the client's difficulties and presenting sessions in supervision.

The content relates to a brief therapy approaching half-way through. The client is a 42-year-old woman who is experiencing blocked grieving after her son was killed in a motorcycle accident. The therapist has listened to the audio recording and has summarised some of the key issues on the *proforma*.

Table 10.2   Example of systematic process notes

Name	Mrs AB	
Therapist	CD	
Session Number	3rd of 8 sessions	
Date	17/02/16	
	Observations	**Hypotheses**
	• *What is said?* • *How is it said?* • *Body language?* • *Metaphors?* • *How do I feel?*	• *Express in everyday language*
Opening of session	The session felt very stilted in the first few minutes.	Were we re-enacting the polite talk of a funeral where emotions are being held in check?
Observation of client	Mrs B was cutting over me whenever I tried to say anything. Her voice sounds very constricted and tight when she talks about 'turning off the life support'	Perhaps struggling to contain feelings of loss? [This sounds to be an important metaphor and she keeps coming back to it – possibly a reference to how she is feeling?]

(Continued)

Table 10.2 (Continued)

Observation of therapist	I am also behaving very 'politely' – keeping everything calm and being almost deferential.	Am I trying to avoid anger directed towards me?
Observation of interaction	She is not looking at me. Long pauses before she speaks. Sighs as though tired.	Tension between us is not really acknowledged perhaps because anger could feel too much for *both* of us.
Progress of core formulation	She is angry at the world and needs an explanation for why her son died. She has been experiencing difficulty swallowing and will not accept that the feelings are part of her unresolved grief.	Looking for explanations outside herself or medical syndromes are a way of avoiding thinking about her bereavement and her guilt that she argued with her son about his choice of partner the night before the crash.
Progress with aims of therapy	The session feels stuck and we are not making progress today as the room seems full of strong feelings but exploration seems blocked.	The session may be reflecting blocked grieving. I have ideas of what might be happening but they feel quite separate from her experience.

Reminders		
Administrative	We are half-way through next week. Check when her son's birthday would have been.	Try to summarise where we are – drawing attention to her feelings about having half the time left – possibly her avoidance of this reflects her difficulty about endings?
Themes to be monitored	• Loss experienced as 'being switched off'. • Her voice constricts when she is experiencing loss.	
Notes for supervision	There is a difficult section at 14 mins 20 secs where she talks about an insensitive doctor who did not seem bothered about the life-support machine being turned off and just wanted to talk about taking her son's organs.	It will be helpful to think through the levels of this: • Is she angry with me for being like the 'doctor'? • Is she saying something about me becoming her life-support? • Is she experiencing me as shut-off or is she telling me she feels shut down? How can I share these ideas with her?

Competence

Understanding how to intervene in different and sometimes demanding contexts is a key ingredient of being a competent therapist. Competence can vary between incompetent (actually causing harm) at one extreme to expert at the other (Hill et al, 1992; Milne et al, 1999). It is important in assessing competence to look at what therapists do rather than what they think they do, so the use of audio recording (or where possible video recording) is crucial.

One approach to developing competence is to look at the ability to stay within model under challenging conditions such as the pressures experienced when a client expresses persistently negative views about the therapy and hostile or derogatory comments about the therapist. These can be developed through role-plays as discussed earlier. With that example an *incompetent* therapist would be paralysed by anxiety, or worse would retaliate and put their own interests ahead of the client's. A *beginner* therapist may try to respond but with defensiveness and little or no awareness of the underlying relationship possibilities. *Increasing competence* may be demonstrated by less defensiveness, but little flexibility and no links to the ongoing formulation of the therapy. A therapist who is *competent*, in contrast, would be flexible and non-defensive but may still not have the overarching skills to then make a link to the overall patterns in the therapy, whereas an *expert* response would go the extra step and be able to sustain a collaborative working style despite sustained hostility, and make meaningful links to ongoing therapy themes in a skilled and effective way.

This approach can be applied to other challenging settings such as a client expressing suicidal ideas, experience of somatic symptoms (pain, dizziness, etc.) and in-session challenges such as conflicts about confidentiality, and managing intrusions into the therapist's private life. Workshop settings where mutual trust is established provide a good setting for developing and assessing one's own skills and competence in these challenging areas.

Supervision

Supervision for PI therapy has many similarities with supervision of other relational therapies in that the setting and development of an atmosphere of curiosity and exploration is crucial. Some professional bodies may require a certain number of supervised hours of practice before independent practice, but here we deal with the key principles that we have found particularly important in supervising PI therapy.

The experience of supervision may be individual or group, but in either format it is important to develop a collegial rather than hierarchical atmosphere, consistent with the idea of a conversation. It is usual to have audio recordings available, where possible, so that the focus of attention can shift easily between the material of the session and the therapist's recall of events. Supervision with Robert Hobson was especially illuminating in listening for the 'minute particulars', sometimes spending 30 minutes listening in detail to a tiny fragment of a session and making hypotheses, developing imaginative capacity and considering alternative ways that the therapist might have intervened. Table 10.3 summarises the main stages in developing the focus of supervision.

Table 10.3 Developing levels of supervision

Level of skill being supervised	Areas requiring supervisor attention	Potential pitfalls for the supervisor
Basic technical competence		
Includes the ability to use all main types of intervention.	Clarifying basic techniques. Ensuring clarity of intervention. Ensuring interventions are in response to appropriate cues.	Avoid moving to complex skills before basic competence is established.
Responsiveness and sensitivity		
includes responsiveness to client need, timing and tact of interventions.	Timing of interventions. Client capacity to deal with emotional distress. Tact and sensitivity of responses including intercultural, gender, disability issues.	Possible to overload the supervisee with more material than can be managed at that stage of development.
Ability to stay in mode under pressure		
Being able to adhere to the model under challenging conditions.	Identifying warning signs of therapist intrusiveness or retaliation when facing challenges from the client.	Need to tolerate uncertainty for both therapist and supervisor.
Formulating material at the session level		
Analytic and synthetic skills.	Identifying narrative structure at a session level.	Imposition of supervisor's views before the therapist has sufficient understanding of the therapeutic process.
Formulating at the case level		
Ensuring there is an overall therapeutic overview.	Identifying appropriate level and type of case level formulation.	Awareness of risk of supervisor carrying out therapy by proxy.

Level of skill being supervised	Areas requiring supervisor attention	Potential pitfalls for the supervisor
Making sense of interpersonal anxiety or tension		
Using re-enactments to therapeutic effect.	Identifying sources of interpersonal anxiety by detailed exploration of sessions.	Awareness of further re-enactment between therapist and supervisor.
	Re-enactments with the therapist of pre-existing patterns.	
	Distinguishing types of counter-transference: concordant and complementary.	
Recognising and feeding back therapist blind spots		
Being aware of therapist's habitual defensive strategies.	Attending to internal cues.	Awareness of possible shame or humiliation for the therapist.
	Receptivity to 'parallel communications' from the client about unacknowledged re-enactments by the therapist	
Recognising blocks in the therapy		
Has therapy become ineffective?	Identifying signs that the therapy has become blocked.	Awareness of therapist fears of negative or critical evaluations by the supervisor.

However, in the early stages of supervision there is usually a focus on making sure that the basic skills are there – identifying possible cues, ensuring the trainee knows what different interventions are like and what alternatives there were. The key areas of focus at this stage are to identify and develop basic techniques and that they are in response to cues from the client. The main risk for the supervisor at this stage is shifting onto other fascinating discussions before the basic skills have been covered.

Later the focus shifts to nuances of the therapy including timing and sensitivity to the client's experience. The main risk for the supervisor here is in overloading the therapist with too much information so they become demoralised. As the therapist progresses the emphasis often shifts to staying within the model when under pressure and it is important then for the therapist to experience the difference between tactically shifting to keep the alliance as good as possible and shifting defensively under pressure. The supervisor at this point may also run the risk of intruding on the supervisee's personal space whilst exploring complex re-enactments.

As competence develops the supervisory focus can settle on the narrative flow within the session and eventually an overview (or in some situations a formulation) of the whole case. The risk for the supervisor here is in running the case 'by proxy', for example by telling the therapist what is happening and what to say rather than leaving space for the therapist to find his or her own 'voice'.

As the therapist matures it is possible to discuss sources of interpersonal anxiety and to include those arising within the therapist. This is a related concept to that of counter-transference. As with psychoanalytic models of therapy the supervisor can help to distinguish counter-transference arising from the re-enactment of a typical pattern of the client's relationships (complementary type) from counter-transference where the therapist picks up and starts to experience feelings of which the client may not yet be fully aware (concordant type).

The therapist should gradually discover his or her own blocks – personal themes that make it difficult for the therapist to 'hear' what is being said. The risk the supervisor faces when identifying these blocks is analogous to the risk for the therapist with the client – the insight may be valid, but if it is said prematurely or insensitively it may cause the client, or in this case, the therapist, to feel exposed or even humiliated.

The supervisor needs to be skilled to help the therapist identify internal cues, and on occasion there may be parallel communications to discuss where the conversation between client and therapist mirrors the conversation between therapist and supervisor. With an appropriately mindful attitude the supervisor can be 'curious' about the parallels allowing further exploration.

Conclusions

This chapter has given a brief account of the teaching methods based on extensive research and presented some suggestions arising from the delivery of training programmes. It should be clear from the discussion in this chapter that we favour a self-directed, and peer-directed, approach to learning wherever possible. When we consider the role of the supervisor or facilitator it should reflect Vygotsky's model of striving to provide the conditions for optimal learning by providing enough conceptual scaffolding for the developing therapist always to be in their zone of proximal development (see Hess et al., 2008; Zonzi et al., 2014); able to reach beyond what they already know by the judicious input from a supervisor, mentor or facilitator, but not paralysed by anxiety.

11

Epilogue

In this last chapter we have included a brief section on Robert Hobson's background and development to put his work, which inspired this book, into context.

Robert F. Hobson

Robert (Bob) Hobson grew up in Rossendale, Lancashire, UK. He was educated at Bacup and Rawtenstall Grammar School; Selwyn College, Cambridge; and Manchester University Medical School where he graduated in medicine in 1941. During his house jobs he worked as a house surgeon in neurosurgery at Manchester Royal Infirmary. Seeing patients with profound brain injury, he was fascinated by the interplay of brain, mind and spirit. From 1944 to 1946 he served as surgeon lieutenant, RNVR (Royal Navy Volunteer Reserve), on the Arctic convoys in the last two years of World War II. This experience gave him a model of how a captain must lead from the front, while also supporting from the rear – something he was to apply regularly in his later work.

He trained in psychiatry at the Maudsley Hospital under Professor Sir Aubrey Lewis and Professor Sir Denis Hill before developing a distinguished career as a psychiatrist. His MD thesis in 1951 was on prognostic factors in electroconvulsive therapy (ECT). In later years, colleagues who knew him as a psychotherapist were amazed to learn that this seminal ECT study was by the same Hobson. His breadth of experience would be difficult to match as he worked extensively in the emerging fields of child and adolescent psychiatry, addiction psychiatry and in forensic psychiatry. He then extended the role of the psychotherapist into community and pastoral developments with a crucial report he wrote for the then Bishop of Southwark, pushing forward the development of pastoral counselling services. He saw psychotherapy as having a contribution beyond the consulting room and gave these ideas practical expression through his work with groups such as the Guild of Pastoral Psychology and Westminster Pastoral Foundation. He counted among his friends several notable theologians, including Michael Ramsey (Lord Ramsey, former Archbishop of Canterbury) and David Jenkins, former Bishop of Durham.

He developed an influential therapeutic community at the Royal Bethlem Hospital, which ran for 20 years, but he warned subsequently of the dangers of being drawn into a 'charismatic leadership' style. As a pioneer in the field, he experienced considerable personal pain when his ideal of the community passed through the inevitable cycles of growth, dissolution, profound despair and rebirth. He was able to link this experience with his former role as Chair of the Jungian Society for Analytical Psychology (where he had qualified as a Jungian analyst in 1954) and his personal meetings with Carl Gustav Jung. These prepared him to see that the cycle of dissolution and rebirth in a therapeutic community was not due to the personal failings of members of staff of that community, but was part of a larger system.

In the 1960s, Hobson pioneered the use of audio and video recordings in clinical supervision, arguing that therapists' recollections of their own work are a poor guide to the minute particulars of the encounter. In a supervision group, he would stop the tape after a therapist statement and ask each member to predict how the patient would respond. This was scientific method in action, as each exposed their predictions (and accompanying rationales) to the risk of Popperian disconfirmation. His tape-based supervision was a direct precursor of subsequent research on strains and ruptures in the therapeutic alliance. It was also during this period that his ideas about a new approach to psychotherapy began to crystallise, and he worked with Russell Meares to elaborate a model based less upon interpretation and more on developing a 'conversation' with someone; a real meeting of heart and mind.

Having achieved so much in a little over 20 years, he surprised many London colleagues by returning to his roots in the north of England in 1974. He shaped psychotherapy training in the north from a base in the Manchester Royal Infirmary with sessions around the region. He ran a small in-patient unit in Gaskell House, shared with Dr Sidney Benjamin. This provided a remarkable experience for a generation of psychiatrists training in Manchester as he showed how his conversational methods applied equally powerfully in getting to know someone admitted for an acute psychosis as for someone admitted from the adjacent psychotherapy clinic.

As the Regional Director for psychotherapy training, he persuaded the then regional training director to let him use the staff training college at Brindle

Lodge for residential courses several times a year. Through those intensive workshops he inspired a group of colleagues to develop advanced training in psychotherapy in the north-west of England. Until a month before his death he continued his work as a supervisor of senior staff in the area. As a supervisor he modelled his own approach to therapy; being actively involved in a supportive but searching conversation about personal experience.

Sometimes he needed to be convinced that he had something worth saying, but a brief selection of his papers outlined below show the remarkable breadth of his interests. He set himself ferociously high standards, but each of his clinical papers, whether on 'Loneliness' (Hobson, 1974: developing the concept of 'aloneness-togetherness') or 'The Messianic Community' (Hobson, 1979: on the risks of the charismatic leader) had a profound influence. Some of his papers drew on his love of literature and he wrote on Coleridge's *The Rime of the Ancient Mariner* (Hobson, 1984) and Arthurian legend (Hobson, 1965) with equal ease. He was proud of his Lancastrian background adding traditional poetry in Lancashire dialect to his immense knowledge of folklore and myth, and he learned Welsh to study Arthurian legends in their original form.

His fullest exposition is his 1985 book *Forms of Feeling: The Heart of Psychotherapy*. Every therapist and counsellor can learn from it. It is intensely personal, immediate, wise, theoretically rich, disarmingly direct and free of jargon, and we draw heavily on that wisdom in this book. *Forms of Feeling* reflects his unique ability to blend personal, literary, scientific, psychodynamic, spiritual and philosophical themes and ideas, together with finely drawn and succinct stories of therapeutic encounters.

It draws freely upon diverse 'schools' of psychotherapy, seeking a dynamic synthesis rather than a mere eclectic compromise. The writing is poetic: every word feels chosen for its textured meanings, resonances and associations, every phrase crafted with intensely applied skill. Unusually for a psychotherapy book, it attracted a positive review by the eminent American cognitive psychologist George A. Miller.

Alongside his direct influence on the psychotherapy research carried out in Britain, which earned him a Lifetime Achievement Award from the UK Chapter of the Society for Psychotherapy Research, Hobson's long-held central ideas and beliefs about how psychotherapy helps people change – through interpersonal learning grounded in a secure, open, responsive, interdependent therapeutic relationship – have proved prescient, as they continue to gain support in the wider research literature. His approach also prefigured the trend toward integration across the different approaches to psychotherapy.

Robert Frederick Hobson, psychiatrist and psychotherapist: born Rawtenstall, Lancashire, 18 May 1920; Physician, Bethlem Royal Hospital 1954–74; Consultant Psychotherapist, Manchester Royal Infirmary 1974–85; Reader in Psychotherapy, Manchester University 1974–85, Honorary Emeritus Reader 1985–99; married 1946 Marjorie Brett (two sons, one daughter); died Stockport, Cheshire, 13 November 1999.

Obituaries:

Margison, F.R., 'Obituary Robert F. Hobson', *Guardian*, Monday 29 November 1999.

Margison, F. and Shapiro, D.A. (2000) 'Obituaries: Robert F. Hobson', *The Psychiatrist (Bulletin of the Royal College of Psychiatrists), 24*: 238.

Shapiro, D.A., 'Obituary Robert F. Hobson', *Independent,* Monday 29 November 1999.

Appendix: The Psychodynamic-Interpersonal Therapy Rating Scale (PITRS)

Introduction

This rating scale is an abbreviated version of the full scale which has more detailed notes for raters. The rating rules are important if it is to be used in research, so that good reliability can be maintained, but for use in learning the model less formality is needed.

The PITRS is an adaptation of the Sheffield Psychotherapy Rating Scale (SPRS), developed by Startup and Shapiro (1993).

Using the manual as an aid to learning the model

The adherence manual can be used as a useful tool to learn the model. Therapists can rate their own recordings or role-plays to determine how in or out of model behaviour they are. It is best to start with the basic skills first, as PI therapists should use these items frequently. It is best not to progress to or focus on the intermediate skills until the basic ones have been mastered.

It can be helpful to listen to portions of recordings, and stop the recording at a point where a PI item has been identified or a PI intervention has been missed. Try to think of ways to improve the PI item, if it gets a low score. If a PI intervention has been missed, stop the recording and try to think of an appropriate high scoring item that the therapist could have said.

The advanced items occur less frequently in therapy than the basic skills. These are harder to learn and are best developed through practice, close supervision and listening and re-listening to one's own therapy recordings.

Specific items

Basic skills

1. Use of statements as opposed to questions
2. Picking up cues

3. Negotiation
4. Understanding hypotheses

Intermediate skills

5. Focusing on feelings (here and now)
6. Metaphor (living symbols)
7. Language of mutuality
8. Linking hypotheses

Advanced skills

9. Explanatory hypotheses
10. Exploratory therapy rationale
11. Sequencing of interventions
12. Relating interpersonal change to therapy
13. Patterns in relationships

Stage 1: Basic skills

1 Statements

Did the therapist use statements as opposed to questions when making an intervention?

1	2	3	4	5	6	7
not at all		some		considerably		extensively

The purpose of this item is to measure the extent to which the therapist's interventions are couched in the form of statements, as opposed to questions. The intention in the model is to promote a feeling language, and the use of statements helps this to develop. Some questions are necessary and the therapist should not be marked down for using questions where it is appropriate (e.g. sorting out a practical issue, arranging a different time to meet or some aspects of a risk assessment). This item should be occurring very frequently throughout the session. A high rating would be achieved if over 80% of the therapist's utterances are in the form of statements.

Examples

The following are examples of interventions that are phrased in the form of statements:

T: It's been a difficult time for you.

T: I imagine it's a struggle to keep going.

T: I wonder perhaps...you could say a bit more.

If the therapist used a lot of questions as opposed to statements he/she would be marked down on this item. The following are examples of interventions that are not in statement form for contrast.

T: How have you been feeling?

T: Why do you think you feel like that?

T: Is it a struggle?

2 Picking up cues

Did the therapist explicitly base his/her interventions on cues (verbal and non-verbal) supplied by the client?

1	2	3	4	5	6	7
not at all		some		considerably		extensively

The purpose of this item is to measure the extent to which the therapist's interventions are explicitly based on verbal and non-verbal cues supplied by the client during the session. These cues include choice of words as well as the content expressed. They also include non-verbal cues such as posture, gestures, facial expression and tone of voice. Cues in the therapist can also be included if the therapist specifically refers to a cue-based response in him/herself. There should be several instances of this item in a session of PI therapy.

Examples

The following are examples of interventions that are explicitly cue-based:

T: As you tell me about what's been happening at home this week, you're looking like you're ready to cry. I suppose you've been feeling pretty desperate about it.

T: And yet, the words you're using to tell me this seem to put a distance between you and what's been happening. Words like 'expectations', 'goals', and so on, as if you feel a bit cut off.

T: It seems you are a bit subdued today...not your normal self.

No doubt there are degrees of explicitness with which a therapist might base his/her interventions. If it seems likely that a given intervention is based on cues provided by the client but it is not certain, then some credit on this item should still be given. In the following example it seems likely that the therapist is referring to something in the client's manner of telling a story, such as the tone of voice or facial expression:

T: There's something sad in those memories.

It may become apparent that the therapist is missing many cues from the client.

C: I've felt so anxious and worried I haven't had a wink of sleep.

T: Can you tell me more about your sleep?

In this example the therapist has missed the verbal cue about the client feeling anxious and worried and instead focuses on the client's sleep. If this is typical of a lot of the session, the therapist would receive a low score.

3 Negotiation

Did the therapist express his/her views concerning the patient's experiences and circumstances as tentative statements, open to correction, and inviting elaboration and feedback?

1	2	3	4	5	6	7
not at all		some		considerably		extensively

This item assesses the 'how' of the therapist's talk. It is concerned with the extent to which the therapist, rather than implying 'this is right', conveys the message, 'I am trying to understand how you are feeling and this is how I think you may be feeling...based upon what you have told me and how you appear...but maybe I am wrong.' To be tentative is not to be vague. Therapist statements in a session rated highly on this item may well be definite (i.e. clearly 'owned' by the therapist) and often specific (i.e. referring to particular experiences and making quite detailed comments or observations concerning these). These qualities of definiteness and specificity follow from the therapist doing his or her best to be accurate, to really attend to the cues from the client and the minute particulars of the conversation. The therapist conveys his or her wish to be corrected, expressing a hope for communication which will lead on to dialogue, with an adjustment of misunderstanding. This wish is expressed in words, constructions and turns of phrase, as well as in the way they are spoken. The rater should watch for such indicators of tentativeness as 'maybe', 'it's almost as if', 'I'm not sure about this, but...', 'I wonder if...', etc. The ideal scenario is when a therapist makes a suggestion, which is then further shaped and modified by the client. There should be several instances of this item in a session.

Examples

The following illustrates a response typical of a therapist scoring very *low* on this scale.

C: I think I've been spending more money lately because I just need to cheer myself up.

T: That's not the best way to cope with feeling down; you have fallen back into behaving like a small child.

A medium rating would be obtained by a therapist using responses similar to the following:

T: I'm not sure about this, but maybe, in a way, when you feel miserable and alone, buying things helps comfort you. It's almost as if you're feeling again like that a child who needs treats, as if having things for yourself helps you feel comforted, and maybe loved.

A high rating is reserved for therapists skilfully adopting the negotiating style in relation to issues within the relationship between therapist and client:

C: That's just it, you see, you don't seem to want me to get over it.

T: That feels pretty important to me. I wonder if what is happening between us...I'm not sure...it feels to me as if you're disappointed, as if you feel I'm not really with you, not really on your side.

C: I thought I was doing really well in the last week. I've got out much more, I've been meeting friends, I've been playing the guitar again.

T: I wonder if it feels when we try to look at what's happening, the huge efforts you are making to change are being ignored by me, and you don't feel valued...I'm not sure...almost that I want you to remain unwell. [Pause]

C: I don't know...

T: How you feel is very important...and it's important to me...to really understand...I wonder if we could stay with that feeling you have...you said...'you don't seem to want me to get over it'.

C: I was looking forward to telling you today what I had achieved in the week, but when I told you...you just seemed disinterested...I was disappointed...

T: Frustrated...annoyed...can we stay with these feelings

C: Very annoyed...

In this example, by adopting a negotiating style, the therapist is able to help the client explore his feelings of anger towards the therapist, whilst deepening the conversation between them.

4 Understanding hypotheses

Did the therapist offer statements of empathic understanding that helped to deepen the conversation?

1	2	3	4	5	6	7
not at all		some		considerably		extensively

This item measures the extent to which the therapist offers empathic and imaginative statements of what he/she feels that the client is experiencing right now in the relationship. Empathy is conveyed in such a way as to call forth a response; to achieve a dialogue with increasing mutual understanding, in which the desire to understand is communicated. This involves more than simple repetition or reflection of the client's message; that something more comes from the therapist's own perspective on the experiences reported by the client, and is derived from the therapist's understanding and best guess of what the client is experiencing. This requires the therapist to pay close attention to cues from the client as to how he/she is feeling. One important aim of understanding hypotheses is often to contribute to the resolution of misunderstanding. Another is to deepen the conversation in a way that feels acceptable and safe for the client. Item 1 (using statements) can also be scored if the hypothesis is couched in the form of a statement. There should be many instances of this item in a session of PI therapy.

Examples

The following is a simple example of an understanding hypothesis that tries to take forward the client's self-awareness, and invites a response:

C: I get really fed up at times and...[client sighs]...I just don't know what to do.

T: Perhaps you are feeling quite unsure...lost?

C: It's like everyone I've known couldn't care less...

The next example is directly concerned with the resolution of misunderstanding.

C: I don't see the point of coming here. My doctor told me to come...but I don't see that talking is going to make any difference. I thought you would be able to actually do something.

T: Mhm...It sounds as if you feel you've been sent here...to see me...under some kind of false pretences...you're understandably feeling aggrieved and frustrated...it wasn't what you had in mind...

C: Yes, well, my wife thinks I should be here...she's worried I'm going to top myself.

Understanding hypotheses are not reflections (when the therapist repeats back to the client what he/she has said). Below is an example of a reflection which is an empathic statement, but it would receive a low score on this item, but a high score on item 1 as it is not a question.

C: I get really fed up at times and...[client sighs]...I just don't know what to do.

T: You get very fed up...

Stage 2: Intermediate skills

5 Focusing on feelings (here and now)

Did the therapist focus on the here and now experience of the client in the session, encouraging the client to stay with feelings to see what comes to mind?

1	2	3	4	5	6	7
not at all		some		considerably		extensively

This item measures the extent to which the therapist promotes the client's experiencing, acknowledgment and recognition of feelings, whether or not these have been expressed, and whether or not the client is aware of them. The therapist must act to promote this awareness, rather than respond to the client's expression of feelings by seeking to explain or dispel them. This encouragement of the client to stay with the experience of a particular situation as it arises during the session may require explicit guidance to the client, using instructions or suggestions. Particularly highly rated are efforts by the therapist to focus on the physical sensations and inner experiences associated with feelings, particularly if these feelings are aroused in relation to specific other people, notably the therapist. There should be several instances of this in a session of PI therapy.

Examples

The following are examples of the therapist focusing on the client's here and now experience:

C: It's just rather frustrating, I suppose, to realise how much time I've spent marking time in a way, not really getting anywhere at work.

T: Let's just stay with that frustration, and try to get in touch with what it makes you feel, inside.

C: You never seem to come out with what you think of what I've said or done, so I just have to try and figure it out for myself. So, yes, I do wonder what you think, and that's not very comfortable.

T: Well I wonder if you could stay with that feeling of discomfort...it's here now...just stay...let's see what comes to mind

C: John said I was wrong to react like I did, but I just couldn't help it, somehow. I just had to tell them that I wasn't in a position to help out yet again, that they'd been taking it for granted that I would, but that it just wasn't possible. It happened again on Tuesday. Bill said that his section were short-staffed, and could I let them have an extra person for the day, despite their already having had extra help the previous day, which is much more than any section would normally ever have in a week.

T: You're feeling pretty tense as you tell me about all this...I wonder if we could stay a bit with how you are feeling inside...right now...

6 Metaphor (living symbols)

Did the therapist encourage and elaborate the client's use of metaphor?

1	2	3	4	5	6	7
not at all		some		considerably		extensively

This item is designed to measure the extent to which the therapist deliberately aims to convey and promote a symbolical attitude. This means endowing words, gestures, dreams, etc., with value – regarding them not only as communications of formulated messages but also as living symbols.

The therapist rated highly on this item encourages the client to use metaphoric communication, and elaborates or builds upon metaphors introduced by the client, in order to make greater integration of the client's experience, and to heighten or intensify the client's experiencing and expression of feelings. However, the rater should be alert to the possible use of metaphor as an adornment rather than as direct and vivid communication. There should be some instances of this item in a session of PI therapy.

Examples

In the following example, the therapist achieves a rating above '1' by the use of figurative language. However, this is not based on the client's material in this session, and so the rating would not be above '2'.

C: There's so much to do at work that I often feel I cannot carry on.

T: You sound to me like Samson or Charles Atlas bearing the world on your shoulders.

The following examples would secure moderate to high ratings on this item, as the therapist promotes the client's use of metaphor, teasing out and elaborating metaphoric content of which the client is scarcely aware:

C: It seems such a heavy burden when I am the one who always has to take responsibility for things.

T: The weight of that burden feels really overwhelming, maybe to the point where you feel crushed by it.

C: I find it very difficult to do my job. There is very little guidance laid down. I'm all at sea with the work, especially at this time of year.

T: No guidance, all at sea. It feels like there's no one to steer you, and you're at the mercy of the waves, buffeted around by the waves, by things you can't control.

C: I don't really feel anything inside...just empty.

T: Empty...a void...that's a powerful image.

C: I do feel that, a chasm, I suppose, opening up between me and everything or everyone around me.

T: A great vastness of the distance between you...

7 Language of mutuality

Did the therapist use the language of shared endeavour ('I' and 'we')?

1	2	3	4	5	6	7
not at all		some		considerably		extensively

This item measures the therapist's use of language conveying his or her full participation in the therapeutic conversation. The use of first-person words 'I' and 'we' affirms the aim of a conversation between two separate and yet related responsible persons who, alone and together, claim their actions. The message of this language is that 'we' are separate people, yet there is a sharing. Use of 'I' and 'we' often has the effect of deepening the conversation as the focus is placed directly on the client–therapist relationship. There should be several instances of this item in any session of PI therapy.

Examples

The following illustrates the therapist's use of 'I' and 'we' to affirm the therapeutic conversation:

T: I feel that what we're coming to grips with, here, is a big part of what happens when you are trying to get to feel closer to someone ...there's a fear... And with that comes...a moving away...a moving away from me...I think ...we can both feel that tension that fear...*now*...

T: When you say that, you look away from me, I feel it would be difficult for you to hold my glance...because of the strong feelings between us.

In contrast, the following would be consistent with a rating of '1', because the therapist avoids using 'I' or 'we'.

T: It sounds as if it was difficult for you to come to the session this morning?

Whereas the statement below would receive a high rating on this item.

T: It sounds as if it was difficult for you to come to see me this morning? It feels that difficulty's between us now…in the room here.

The use of 'you' can have a rating above '1' on this item if this is accompanied by use of 'I' and 'we':

T: This is a big part of what happens when you try to get close to someone, you both want it and yet, I feel as we're talking together, we're finding it pretty scary, too.

8 Linking hypotheses

Did the therapist link the client's present feelings with feelings in other contexts and at other times, with the central link being between each of these and the 'here and now' of the therapeutic relationship?

1	2	3	4	5	6	7
not at all		some		considerably		extensively

This item measures the therapist's use of observed recurrent patterns in the client's experiences and behaviour to make links and draw parallels, using a tentative style. The therapist helps the client to make sense of experiences by creating greater cohesion and thus to counter fragmentation and loss of integration. Links may be (a) between events within therapy at different times: perhaps during one interview, perhaps relating what is happening now to previous sessions; or (b) between patterns in the present therapeutic conversation and those in other areas of life (especially ways in which relationships are defective and distorted). This item would receive a '1' if there is no reference to the therapy or the therapeutic relationship. Instead a link between relationships that did not include the therapist–client relationship would be rated under item 13 (Patterns in relationships). There should be some examples of this item in a session of PI therapy.

Examples

The following example would yield a high rating, because the therapist made links between patterns in the therapeutic relationship and those in other areas of life.

C: I really find it difficult when he asks me about my movements over the next few days. He seems to want to tie me down, and that annoys me. I just wish he wouldn't hassle me so much, and just let me decide for myself how to allocate my time.

T: This feeling of being hassled by your boss reminds me, in a way, of what happens here, when you feel I'm trying to tie you down too, when I want to know how you're feeling about things. You seem to find it really hard, and to get pretty uptight and angry, whenever someone, perhaps especially someone with power or authority, wants something from you.

Stage 3: Advanced skills

9 Explanatory hypotheses

Did the therapist introduce possible reasons or explanations for the client's behaviour and experiences, particularly in respect of disturbances in relationships within and outside therapy?

1	2	3	4	5	6	7
not at all		some		considerably		extensively

This item refers to an intervention by the therapist that offers a reason or some form of explanation as to the basis of the client's feelings or behaviour. It rarely occurs as a stand alone intervention but often follows a series of linking or understanding hypotheses. The term hypothesis implies that the therapist should present it in a tentative fashion to be agreed, modified or rejected by the client.

Often there is reference to a present action that is carried out in order to avoid a particular kind of relationship that would result in some catastrophe or feared outcome. This fear of catastrophe may or may not be completely outside awareness. In the conversation, it may or may not be explicitly linked with past experience (like 'I was abandoned by my mum'). It is desirable that the client should contribute some or all of the explanation themselves, so that client contributions to this are 'credited' to the therapist in making the rating, provided that there is evidence that the therapist has contributed to the client's arrival at the explanation. This item does not occur frequently in a session and may not be present in every session of PI therapy.

Examples

To aid rating, consider four ways in which therapists may attempt to explain the client's current issues:

(1) Fears of intimacy and abandonment

T: So although you would really like to feel close to someone, you're scared of getting close and find yourself often running from the possibility of an intimate relationship.

(2) Events or motives rooted in the client's past

T: I wonder if your indecisiveness regarding the possibility of separating from your wife is in some way connected to that deeper conflict we've talked about – the trouble you had earlier in your life around leaving your home and your mother.

(3) Basic patterns which influence the client's reactions to the therapist

T: You feel cross now and frustrated...with me...[pause]...and a pressure from me...and we have talked a lot about how angry you feel with your father because he was constantly making demands...I wonder if these feelings are connected in some way...and you feel I am making demands on you...

(4) Motives or tendencies which serve to reduce anxiety or avoid warded off feelings

T: It's hard to face things we are scared of...very hard...it feels sometimes...that you are a bit afraid of showing a bit more of yourself to me...the inside you...maybe because...there's a fear...that I won't like you...with that fear...comes a feeling of not being likeable...I wonder...and that seems to stem from...the very difficult times when you were little...and were constantly told how bad and horrible you were.

Note that reasons or causes deriving from the client's thought patterns do *not* increase ratings on this item, unless reference is made to origins of those thought patterns in emotions, problematic or conflictual motives, or relationships with others. Thus, the following example is compatible with a rating of '1' for the session:

T: You are thinking about this in very negative terms. I have noticed a general tendency you have to blame yourself when things go wrong, and yet never to take the credit when things go well.

If the therapist were to proceed to link the problematic thought pattern to emotions, motives or relationships, however, then a medium rating would be achieved.

T: You are thinking about this in very negative terms. I have noticed a general tendency you have to blame yourself when things go wrong, and yet never to take the credit when things go well. Perhaps this goes back a long way, and maybe it relates to the way your parents seemed to judge you quite harshly at times...I'm not sure.

A high rating would be to give explanations that include some aspect of the therapeutic relationship.

T: You are thinking about this in very negative terms. I think you have a tendency to blame yourself when things go wrong, and yet never to take the credit when things go well. Perhaps this goes back a long way, and maybe it relates to the way your parents seemed to judge you quite harshly at times...and maybe it explains last week when we had that mix up...you felt you were to blame...but it was really probably to do with both of us getting mixed up...

10 Exploratory therapy rationale

Did the therapist provide a rationale which suggested that working on understanding and changing the client's characteristic patterns of feeling and action in relationships, would help overcome the client's difficulties and symptoms?

1	2	3	4	5	6	7
not at all		some		considerably		extensively

The purpose of this item is to measure how extensively the therapist discussed the importance of focusing on relationships, especially the therapeutic relationship, for the purpose of overcoming the client's problems. This connection need not have been explicit, but it must have been strongly implied. This item should be present in the initial sessions of a PI therapy, and may occur again through the course of the therapy, but may not be present in every session.

Examples

The following is an example of a therapist statement that should receive a medium rating as there is an implied link between relationships and the client's depressive symptoms. A high rating would be given if there was a specific link to the therapeutic relationship:

T: Since so much of what's happening with you at the moment has to do with your relationships with other people, I think that as you begin to understand and work out some of those things, you will feel less depressed.

In the following example, the rationale offered by the therapist explicitly refers to the therapeutic relationship and so secures a high rating:

T: Since so much of what's happening with you at the moment has to do with your relationships with other people, I think that as you begin to understand and work out some of those things, especially as they come up between us, you will feel less depressed.

11 Sequencing of interventions

Did the therapist present interventions within a given episode in the sequence of staying with feelings => thoughts/symbolic material => relationships?

1	2	3	4	5	6	7
not at all		some		considerably		extensively

This item should occur repeatedly over the course of a therapy although not always in its entirety. The therapist should be encouraging the client to access or focus on feelings and working then from that point with the material that develops. This material usually involves a connection with relationships at some level. The sequencing may sometimes involve an explanation at the end in the form of an explanatory hypothesis, but this is less frequent.

The main emphasis in rating should be on the therapist abstaining from offering causes or reasons for a behaviour or experience without first facilitating, experiencing in the here and now, and staying with that experience, which may then lead on to relationships.

Examples

The following illustrates material that should be rated low on this item:

C: I don't feel like talking today, it just feels too much of an effort.

T: Maybe that's because you don't want to get involved with the difficult feelings we talked about last time.

A higher rating would be given if the therapist responded as follows, interposing an empathic reflection before proceeding to offer an explanation:

C: I don't feel like talking today, it just feels too much of an effort.

T: Mhmm, you are feeling weary... [feelings]

C: Yeah...fed up...

T: Errr...I can feel that you do [gesturing with her hands] ...it's palpable...I wonder if you could stay with this feeling...fed up...weary...stuck...can't be bothered... [staying with feelings]

C: [Sighs] It feels really hard to get started today. I've had a lot of bad dreams in the last week. About dying...and dead bodies...horrible... [thoughts, symbolic material]

T: Umh...dying...we spent most of last week talking about your mum's death...I know you found that very hard...I wonder if you feel that discussion between us has stirred things up in you...fears...nightmares... [relationship with mother]

In the above example there is a clear sequence of staying with a feeling – seeing what emerges – and then linking that to a problematic relationship.

The therapist would receive a low rating if he/she attempted to explore and provide an explanation without this arising from an initial focus on feelings. This kind of intervention is not using feeling language and is an intellectual approach to the problem. The principles of this item are most readily demonstrated at the microscopic level. However, in rating a session on this item, at least as much attention should be paid to larger units of analysis. During an episode (i.e. a portion of the session devoted to a single topic or closely related set of topics or issues) lasting several minutes or even taking up a substantial proportion of the hour, the therapist's activities may shift between staying with feelings, symbolic material, relationships and explanatory activities.

12 Relating interpersonal change to therapy

Did the therapist relate changes in the client's interpersonal relationships to the emphasis in therapy on understanding and changing the client's ways of relating to others, including in particular the therapist?

1	2	3	4	5	6	7
not at all		some		considerably		extensively

In order for this item to be rated greater than '1', the therapist must have made a connection between the focus on relationships in therapy and changes that have occurred in the client's relationships. This item will not occur in all sessions of PI therapy.

Examples

The following is an example of the therapist having clearly related interpersonal change to therapy. This example would warrant a medium to high rating depending on how this discussion continued.

T: We've spent a lot of our time together looking at your relationship with your wife and on some of the things that were making it hard for you to spend more time with your children. These relationships seem to be very much better for you now than when you first came here. It seems to me that our looking at these issues together has helped you feel quite different about them. I'm wondering how much you feel this too.

The following example should be rated medium on this item because the therapist helped the client to relate what was discussed in therapy to her resolution of a specific relationship problem. It does not get a very high rating as it is not related to the 'here and now' or the therapist–client relationship.

T: Last week we discussed a problem you were having with your brother. I'd like to know how you're feeling about him now.

C: I do feel it's a bit easier to talk to him now, somehow he doesn't irritate me as much as he did before.

T: When we talked about him last week, you seemed to come to realise that it wasn't so much what he said that got to you, as how you felt he was trying to carry on controlling you the way your dad did when you were little. Maybe that new way of looking at it has made it easier to feel OK with him.

Were the previous example to include reference to work done on the client–therapist relationship, it would warrant a higher rating:

T: Last week we discussed a problem you were having with your brother, and how a similar problem came up between us as we were looking at how you felt about him. You've spent some time with him this week.

C: I do feel it's a bit easier to talk to him now. Somehow he doesn't irritate me as much as he did before.

T: When we talked about him last week, you seemed to come to realise that it wasn't so much what he said that got to you, as how you felt he was trying to carry on controlling you the way your dad did when you were little. And our conversation seemed to be going in much the same way, with you feeling that I was a bit controlling...perhaps which reminded you a bit of how it was with your dad...Maybe that new way of looking at it has made it easier to feel OK with me, and with your brother too.

13 Patterns in relationships

Did the therapist draw parallels or point out patterns in two or more of the client's relationships for the purpose of helping the client understand how she/he functions in interpersonal relationships?

1	2	3	4	5	6	7
not at all		some		considerably		extensively

The purpose of this item is to measure the extent to which the therapist helps the client explore past or present relationships for the purpose of identifying patterns which occur in two or more of those relationships. This item may not occur in all sessions of PI therapy.

Examples

The following are examples in which the therapist pointed out a pattern in the client's relationships (Example (a)) and a parallel between two of the client's relationships (Example (b)).

(a) T: It appears to have been very easy for you, both in your present relationship and in [past significant other relationships], to bend to meet the other person's needs and to neglect yourself.

(b) C: I really get angry when my friend starts telling me what to do. Whenever we get together she has advice for me on how I ought to do this or how I ought to do that.

T: That sounds similar to the reaction you have when your boyfriend gives you advice. It might be helpful for us to understand a bit more about that.

The parallels and links yielding high ratings for this item – 'Patterns in relationships' – need make no reference to the therapeutic relationship. If a link is made between a pattern in one of the client's relationships and the therapeutic relationship, the item 'Linking hypotheses' should also be scored more than '1'.

Psychodynamic-Interpersonal Therapy Rating Scale

Basic skills

1. **STATEMENTS:** Did the therapist use statements as opposed to questions when making an intervention?

1	2	3	4	5	6	7
not at all		some		considerably		extensively

2. **PICKING UP CUES**: Did the therapist explicitly base his/her interventions on cues (verbal and non-verbal) supplied by the client?

1	2	3	4	5	6	7
not at all		some		considerably		extensively

3. **NEGOTIATING STYLE**: Did the therapist express his/her views concerning the patient's experiences and circumstances as tentative statements, open to correction, and inviting elaboration and feedback?

1	2	3	4	5	6	7
not at all		some		considerably		extensively

4. **UNDERSTANDING HYPOTHESES**: Did the therapist offer statements of empathic understanding that helped to deepen the conversation?

1	2	3	4	5	6	7
not at all		some		considerably		extensively

Intermediate skills

5. **FOCUSING ON FEELINGS:** Did the therapist focus on the **HERE AND NOW** experience of the client in the session, encouraging the client to stay with feelings to see what comes to mind?

1	2	3	4	5	6	7
not at all		some		considerably		extensively

6. **METAPHOR**: Did the therapist encourage and elaborate the client's use of metaphor?

1	2	3	4	5	6	7
not at all		some		considerably		extensively

7. **LANGUAGE OF MUTUALITY**: Did the therapist use the language of shared endeavour ('I' and 'we')?

1	2	3	4	5	6	7
not at all		some		considerably		extensively

8. **LINKING HYPOTHESES**: Did the therapist link the client's present feelings with feelings in other contexts and at other times, with the central link being between each of these and the 'here and now' of the therapeutic relationship?

1	2	3	4	5	6	7
not at all		some		considerably		extensively

Advanced skills

9. **EXPLANATORY HYPOTHESES**: Did the therapist introduce possible reasons for the client's behaviour and experiences, particularly in respect of disturbances in relationships within and outside therapy?

1	2	3	4	5	6	7
not at all		some		considerably		extensively

10. **EXPLORATORY THERAPY RATIONALE**: Did the therapist provide a rationale which suggested that working on understanding and changing the client's characteristic patterns of feeling and action in relationships would help overcome the client's difficulties and symptoms?

1	2	3	4	5	6	7
not at all		some		considerably		extensively

11. **SEQUENCING OF INTERVENTIONS**: Did the therapist present interventions within a given episode in the sequence of: staying with feelings => thoughts/symbolic material => relationships?

1	2	3	4	5	6	7
not at all		some		considerably		extensively

12. **RELATING INTERPERSONAL CHANGE TO THERAPY**: Did the therapist relate changes in the client's interpersonal relationships to the emphasis in therapy on understanding and changing the client's ways of relating to others, including in particular the therapist?

1	2	3	4	5	6	7
not at all		some		considerably		extensively

13. **PATTERNS IN RELATIONSHIPS**: Did the therapist draw parallels or point out patterns in two or more of the client's relationships for the purpose of helping the client understand how she/he functions in interpersonal relationships?

1	2	3	4	5	6	7
not at all		some		considerably		extensively

References

Agnew, R.M., Harper, H., Shapiro, D.A. and Barkham, M. (1994) 'Resolving a challenge to the therapeutic relationship: A single-case study', *British Journal of Medical Psychology, 67*: 155–70.

Agnew-Davies, R., Stiles, W.B., Hardy, G.E., Barkham, M. and Shapiro, D.A. (1998) 'Alliance structure assessed by Agnew Relationship Measure (ARM)', *British Journal of Clinical Psychology, 37*: 155–72.

Aspland, H., Llewelyn, S., Hardy, G.E., Barkham, M. and Stiles, W.B. (2008) 'Alliance ruptures and rupture resolution in cognitive-behavior therapy: A preliminary task analysis', *Psychotherapy Research, 18*: 699–710.

Bancroft, J., Skrimshaw, A., Casson, J., Harvard-Watts, O. and Reynolds, K. (1977) 'People who deliberately poison or injure themselves: Their problems and their contacts with helping agencies', *Psychological Medicine, 7*: 289–303.

Barkham, M. (1989) 'Exploratory therapy in two-plus-one sessions: I – Rationale for a brief psychotherapy model', *British Journal of Psychotherapy, 6*: 81–8.

Barkham, M., Hardy, G.E. and Shapiro, D.A. (2011) 'The Sheffield–Leeds psychotherapy research program'. In J.C. Norcross, G.R. VandenBos and D.K. Freedheim (eds), *History of Psychotherapy: Continuity and Change* (2nd edition). Washington, DC: APA, pp. 382–8.

Barkham, M. and Hobson, R.F. (1989) 'Exploratory therapy in two-plus-one-sessions: II – A single case study', *British Journal of Psychotherapy, 6*: 89–100.

Barkham, M. and Margison, F. (2007) 'Practice-based evidence as a complement to evidence-based practice: From dichotomy to chiasmus'. In C. Freeman and M. Power (eds), *Handbook of Evidence-Based Psychotherapies: A Guide for Research and Practice*. Chichester: Wiley, pp. 443–76.

Barkham, M., Margison, F., Leach, C., Lucock, M., Mellor-Clark, J., Evans, C., Benson, L., Connell, J., Audin, K. and McGrath, G. (2001) 'Service profiling and outcomes benchmarking using the CORE-OM: Toward practice-based evidence in the psychological therapies', *Journal of Consulting and Clinical Psychology, 69*: 184–96.

Barkham, M., Rees, A., Shapiro, D.A., Stiles, W.B., Agnew, R.M., Halstead, J., Culverwell, A. and Harrington, V.M.G. (1996) 'Outcomes of time-limited psychotherapy in applied settings: Replicating the Second Sheffield Psychotherapy Project', *Journal of Consulting and Clinical Psychology, 64*: 1079–85.

Barkham, M., Rees, A., Stiles, W.B., Hardy, G.E., and Shapiro, D.A. (2002) 'Dose–effect relations for psychotherapy of mild depression: A quasi-experimental comparison of effects of 2, 8, and 16 sessions', *Psychotherapy Research, 12*: 463–74.

Barkham, M., Rees, A., Stiles, W.B., Shapiro, D.A., Hardy, G.E. and Reynolds, S. (1996) 'Dose effect relations in time-limited psychotherapy for depression', *Journal of Consulting and Clinical Psychology, 64*: 927–35.

Barkham, M., Shapiro, D. A., Hardy, G.E. and Rees, A., (1999) 'Psychotherapy in two-plus-one sessions: Outcomes of a randomized controlled trial of cognitive-behavioral and psychodynamic-interpersonal therapy for sub-syndromal depression', *Journal of Consulting and Clinical Psychology, 67*: 201–11.

Barkham, M., Stiles, W.B. and Shapiro, D.A. (1993). 'The shape of change: Longitudinal assessment of personal problems', *Journal of Consulting and Clinical Psychology, 61*: 667–77.

Buber, M. (1958) *I and Thou* (translated by R.G. Smith). New York: Scribner.

Burns, A., Guthrie, E., Marino-Francis, F., Busby, C., Morris, J., Russell, E., Margison, F., Lennon, S. and Byrne, J. (2005) 'Brief psychotherapy in Alzheimer's disease', *British Journal of Psychiatry, 187*: 143–7.

Castonguay, L.G., Barkham, M., Lutz, W. and McAleavey, A.A. (2013) 'Practice-oriented research: Approaches and applications', In M.J. Lambert (ed.), *Bergin and Garfield's Handbook of Psychotherapy and Behavior Change* (6th edition). New York: Wiley & Sons, pp. 85–133.

Chow, D.L., Miller, S.D., Seidel, J.A., Kane, R.T., Thornton, J.A. and Andrews, W.P. (2015) 'The role of deliberate practice in the development of highly effective psycho-therapists', *Psychotherapy, 52*: 337–45.

Creed, F., Barsky, A. and Leiknes, K.A. (2011) 'Epidemiology: Prevalence, causes and consequences'. In F. Creed, P. Henningsen and P. Fink (eds), *Medically Unexplained Symptoms, Somatisation and Bodily Distress.* Cambridge: Cambridge University Press, pp. 1–42.

Creed, F., Fernandes, L., Guthrie, E., Palmer, S., Ratcliffe, J., Read, N., Rigby, C., Thompson, D. and Tomenson, B. (2003) 'North of England IBS Research Group. The cost-effectiveness of psychotherapy and paroxetine for severe irritable bowel syndrome', *Gastroenterology, 124:* 303–17.

Creed, F., Guthrie, E., Ratcliffe, J., Fernandes, L., Rigby, C., Tomenson, B., Read, N. and Thompson, D.G. (2005) 'Reported sexual abuse predicts impaired functioning but a good response to psychological treatments in patients with severe irritable bowel syndrome'. *Psychosomatic Medicine, 67:* 490–9.

Creed, F., Tomenson, B., Guthrie, E., Ratcliffe, J., Fernandes, Read, N., Palmer, S. and Thompson, D.G. (2008) 'The relationship between somatisation and outcome in patients with severe irritable bowel syndrome', *Journal of Psychosomatic Research, 64*: 613–20.

Detert, N.B., Llewelyn, S.P., Hardy, G.E., Barkham, M., & Stiles, W.B. (2006) 'Assimilation in good- and poor-outcome cases of very brief psychotherapy for mild depression: An initial comparison', *Psychotherapy Research, 16*: 393–407.

Elkin, I., Shea, M.T., Watkins, J.T., Imber, S.D., Sotsy, S.M., Collins, J.F., Glass, D.R., Pilkonis, P.A., Leber, W.R., Docherty, J.P., Fiester, S.J. and Parloff, M.B. (1989) 'National Institute of Mental Health Treatment of Depression Collaborative Research Program. General effectiveness of treatments', *Archives of General Psychiatry, 46*: 971–82.

Elliott, R. (1985) 'Helpful and non-helpful events in brief counselling interviews: An empirical taxonomy'. *Journal of Counseling Psychology, 32*: 307–22.

Elliott, R., Hill, C.E., Stiles, W.B., Friedlander, M.L., Mahrer, A.R. and Margison, F.R. (1987) 'Primary therapist response modes: Comparison of six rating systems', *Journal of Consulting and Clinical Psychology, 55*: 218–23.

Elliott, R., Shapiro, D.A., Firth-Cozens, J., Stiles, W.B., Hardy, G.E., Llewelyn, S.P. and Margison, F.R. (1994) 'Comprehensive process analysis of insight events in cognitive-behavioral and psychodynamic-interpersonal psychotherapies', *Journal of Counseling Psychology, 41*: 449–63.

Ericsson, K.A. and Lehmann, A.C. (1996) 'Expert and exceptional performance: Evidence of maximal adaptation to task', *Annual Review of Psychology, 47*: 273–305.

Evans, C., Connell, J., Barkham, M., Margison, F., McGrath, G., Mellor-Clark, J. and Audin, K. (2002) 'Towards a standardised brief outcome measure: Psychometric properties and utility of the CORE-OM', *British Journal of Psychiatry, 180:* 51–60.

Field, S.D., Barkham, M., Shapiro, D.A. and Stiles W.B. (1994) 'Assessment of assimilation in psychotherapy: A quantitative case study of problematic experiences with a significant other', and *Journal of Counseling Psychology, 41*: 397–406.

Firth, M.T., Huxley, P.J., Oliver, P.J.P. and Margison, F. (1993) 'Quantifying creative encounters: The bumpy road to evaluating psychodynamic training', *Journal of Social Work Practice, 7*: 63–72.

Firth, M.T., Moss, S. and Margison, F.R. (1999) 'Quantifying creative encounters: Part two', *Journal of Social Work Practice, 13*: 93–101.

Fordham, M. (1979) 'Analytical psychology and countertransference', *Contemporary Psychoanalysis, 15:* 630–46.

Glover, G., Webb, M. and Evison, F. (2010) *Improving Access to Psychological Therapies: A Review of the Progress made by Sites in the First Roll-out Year.* North East Public Health Observatory.

Goldberg, D.P., Hobson, R.F., Maguire, G.P., Margison, F.R., O'Dowd, T., Osborn, M.S. and Moss, S. (1984) 'The clarification and assessment of a method of psychotherapy', *British Journal of Psychiatry, 114*: 567–75.

Goldfried, M.R., Castonguay, L.G., Hayes, A.M., Drozd, J.F. and Shapiro, D.A. (1997) 'A comparative analysis of the therapeutic focus in cognitive-behavioral and psychodynamic-interpersonal sessions', *Journal of Consulting and Clinical Psychology, 65:* 740–8.

Greenberg, J. and Mitchell, S. (1983) *Object Relations in Psychoanalytic Theory.* Cambridge, MA: Harvard University Press.

Guthrie, E., Barlow, J., Fernandes, L., Ratcliffe, J., Read, N., Thompson, D.G., Tomenson, B. and Creed, F. (2004a) 'North of England IBS Research Group. Changes in tolerance to rectal distension correlate with changes in psychological state in patients with severe irritable bowel syndrome', *Psychosomatic Medicine, 66*: 578–82.

Guthrie, E., Creed, F.H., Dawson, D.A. and Tomenson, B. (1991) 'A controlled trial of psychological treatment for the irritable bowel syndrome', *Gastroenterology, 100*: 450–7.

Guthrie, E., Kapur, N., Mackway-Jones, K., Chew-Graham, C., Moorey, J., Mendel, E., Marino-Francis, F., Sanderson, S., Turpin, C., Boddy, G. and Tomenson, B. (2001) 'Randomised controlled trial of brief psychological intervention after deliberate self-poisoning', *British Medical Journal, 323*: 135–8.

Guthrie, E., Margison, F.R., Mackay, H., Chew-Graham, C., Moorey, J. and Sibbald, B. (2004b) 'Effectiveness of psychodynamic interpersonal therapy training for primary care counselors', *Psychotherapy Research, 14*: 161–75.

Guthrie, E., Moorey, J., Margison, F.R., Barker, H., Palmer, S., McGrath, G., Tomenson, B. and Creed, F. (1999a) 'Cost-effectiveness of brief psychodynamic-interpersonal therapy in high utilizers of psychiatric services', *Archives of General Psychiatry, 56*: 519–26.

Guthrie, E., Wells, A. and Pilgrim, H. (1999b). 'The Manchester bombing: Providing a rational response', *Journal of Mental Health, 8*: 149–57.

Hall, J., Caleo, S., Stevenson, J. and Meares, R. (2001) 'An economic analysis of psychotherapy for borderline personality disorder patients', *Journal of Mental Health Policy Economics, 4*: 3–8.

Hamilton, J., Guthrie, E., Creed, F., Thompson, D. and Tomenson, B. (2000) 'A randomized controlled trial of psychotherapy in chronic functional dyspepsia', *Gastroenterology, 119*: 661–9.

Hardy, G.E., Aldridge, J., Davidson, C., Rowe, C., Reilly, S. and Shapiro, D.A. (1999) 'Therapist responsiveness to client attachment styles and issues observed in client-identified significant events in psychodynamic-interpersonal psychotherapy', *Psychotherapy Research, 9*: 36–53.

Hardy, G.E. and Barkham, M. (1994) 'The relationship between interpersonal styles and work difficulties', *Human Relations, 47*: 263–81.

Hardy, G.E., Barkham, M., Shapiro, D.A., Reynolds, S., Rees, A. and Stiles, W.B. (1995a) 'Credibility and outcome of cognitive-behavioural and psychodynamic-interpersonal psychotherapy', *British Journal of Clinical Psychology, 34*: 555–69.

Hardy, G.E., Barkham, M., Shapiro, D.A., Stiles, W.B., Rees, A. and Reynolds, S. (1995b) 'Impact of Cluster C personality disorders on the outcome of contrasting psychological treatment for depression', *Journal of Clinical and Consulting Psychology, 63*: 997–1004.

Hardy, G.E., Rees, A., Barkham, M., Shapiro, D.A., Field, S.D. and Elliott, R. (1998a) 'Whingeing versus working': Comprehensive Process Analysis of a vague awareness event', *Psychotherapy Research, 8*: 334–53.

Hardy, G.E. and Shapiro, D.A. (1985) 'Therapist response modes in Prescriptive vs. Exploratory psychotherapy', *British Journal of Clinical Psychology, 24*: 235–45.

Hardy, G.E., Shapiro, D.A, Stiles, W.B. and Barkham, M, (1998b) 'When and why does cognitive-behavioural treatment appear more effective than psychodynamic-interpersonal treatment? Discussion of the findings from the Second Sheffield Psychotherapy Project', *Journal of Mental Health, 2*: 179–90.

Hardy, G.E., Stiles, W.B., Barkham, M. and Startup, M. (1998c) 'Therapist responsiveness to client interpersonal styles during time-limited treatments for depression', *Journal of Consulting and Clinical Psychology, 66*: 304–14.

Hausterier-Wiehle, C., Schneider, G., Lee, S., Sumithipala, A. and Creed, F. (2011) 'Gender, lifespan and cultural aspects'. In F. Creed, P. Henningsen and P. Fink (eds), *Medically Unexplained Symptoms, Somatisation and Bodily Distress*. Cambridge: Cambridge University Press, pp. 132–57.

Henningsen, P., Fink, P., Hausteiner-Wiehle, C. and Rief, W. (2011) 'Terminology, classification and concepts'. In F. Creed, P. Henningsen and P. Fink (eds), *Medically Unexplained Symptoms, Somatisation and Bodily Distress*. Cambridge: Cambridge University Press, pp. 43–68.

Hess, A.K., Hess, C.E, and Hess, J.H. (2008) 'Interpersonal approaches to psychotherapy supervision: A Vygotskyian perspective'. In A.K. Hess, K.D. Hess and T.H. Hess (eds), *Psychotherapy Supervision: Theory, Research and Practice* (2nd edition). Hoboken, NJ: John Wiley & Sons.

Hill, C.E. and O'Grady, K.E. (1985) 'List of therapist intentions illustrated in a case study and with therapists of varying theoretical orientations', *Journal of Counseling Psychology, 32*: 3–22.

Hill, C.E., O'Grady, K.E. and Elkin, I. (1992) 'Applying the Collaborative Study Psychotherapy Rating Scale to rate therapist adherence in cognitive-behavior therapy, interpersonal therapy, and clinical management', *Journal of Consulting and Clinical Psychology, 60*: 73–9.

Hobson, R.F. (1965) *'The King who will return'*, London: Guild of Pastoral Psychology (Guild lecture No. 130).

Hobson, R.F. (1971) 'Imagination and amplification in psychotherapy', *Journal of Analytical Psychology, 16*: 79–105.

Hobson, R.F. (1974). 'Loneliness', *Journal of Analytic Psychology, 19*: 71–89.

Hobson, R.F. (1979) 'The messianic community.' In R. Hinshelwood and N. Manning (eds), *Therapeutic Communities: Reflections and Progress*. London: Routledge & Kegan Paul, pp. 231–44.

Hobson, R. F. (1984) 'The curse in the dead man's eye', *Changes, 2*: 40–44.

Hobson, R.F. (1985) *Forms of Feeling; The Heart of Psychotherapy*. New York: Basic Books.

Hobson, R.P. (2016) *Brief Psychoanalytic Therapy*. Oxford: Oxford University Press.

Hollanders, H. (2000) 'Eclecticism/integrative psychotherapy: Historical developments'. In S. Palmer and R. Woolfe (eds), *Integrative and Eclectic Counselling and Psychotherapy*. London: Sage, pp. 1–30.

Holmes, J. (1996) *Attachment, Intimacy and Autonomy*. New York: Aronson.

Howard, K.I., Kopta, S.M., Krause, M.S. and Orlinsky, D.E. (1986) 'The dose-effect relationship in psychotherapy', *American Psychologist, 41*: 159–64.

Howlett, S. and Guthrie, E. (2001) 'Use of farewell letters in the context of brief psychodynamic-interpersonal therapy with irritable bowel syndrome', *British Journal of Psychotherapy, 18*: 52–67.

Ivey, A.E., Normington, C.J., Miller, C.D., Morrill, W.H. and Haase, R.F. (1968) 'Microcounselling and attending behaviour: An approach to pre-practicum counselor training', *Journal of Counseling Psychology, 15*: 1–12.

Johnstone, L.J., Whomsley, S., Cole, S. and Oliver, N. (2011) *Good Practice Guidelines on the Use of Psychological Formulation*. Leicester: British Psychological Society.

Kagan, N. (1980) 'Influencing human interaction: eighteen years with IPR'. In A.K. Hess (ed.), *Psychotherapy Supervision: Theory, Research, and Practice*. New York: Wiley, pp. 262–83.

Kerr, S., Goldfried, M., Hayes, A., Castonguay, L. and Goldsamt, L. (1992) 'Interpersonal and Intrapersonal Focus in cognitive-behavioral and psychodynamic-interpersonal therapies: A preliminary analysis of the Sheffield Project', *Psychotherapy Research, 2*: 266–76.

Korner, A., Gerull, F., Meares, R. and Stevenson J. (2006) 'Borderline personality disorder treated with the conversational model: A replication study', *Comprehensive Psychiatry, 47*: 406–11.

Korner, A., Gerull, F., Meares, R. and Stevenson, J. (2008) 'The nothing that is something: Core dysphoria as the central feature of borderline personality disorder. Implications for treatment', *American Journal of Psychotherapy, 62*: 377–94.

Layard, R., Clark, D., Bell, S., Knapp, M., Meacher, B., Priebe, S., Turnberg, L., Thornicroft, G. and Wright, B. (2006) 'The depression report: A new deal for depression and anxiety disorders', *The Centre for Economic Performance's Mental Health Policy Group*. London: London School of Economics.

Leiman, M. (1997) 'Procedures as dialogical sequences: A revised version of the fundamental concept in cognitive analytic therapy', *British Journal of Medical Psychology, 70*: 193–207.

Llewelyn, S.P., Elliott, R.K., Shapiro, D.A., Hardy, G.E. and Firth-Cozens, J.A. (1988) 'Client perceptions of significant events in Prescriptive and Exploratory periods of individual therapy', *British Journal of Clinical Psychology, 27*: 105–14.

Loranger, A.W., Sartorius, N., Andreoli, A., Berger, P., Channabasavanna, S.M., Coid, B., et al. (1994) 'The international personality disorder examination (IPDE): The World Health Organization/alcohol, drug abuse, and mental health administration international pilot study of personality disorders', *Archives of General Psychiatry, 51*: 215–24.

Mace, C. and Margison, F.R. (1997) 'Attachment and psychotherapy: An overview', *British Journal of Medical Psychology, 70*: 209–15.

Mackay, H.C., Barkham, M. and Stiles, W.B. (1998) 'Staying with the feeling: An anger event in psychodynamic-interpersonal therapy', *Journal of Counseling Psychology, 45*: 279–89.

Mackay, H.C., Barkham, M., Stiles, W.B. and Goldfried, M.R. (2002) 'Patterns of client emotion in helpful sessions of cognitive-behavioral and psychodynamic-interpersonal therapy', *Journal of Counseling Psychology, 49*: 376–80.

Madill, A. and Barkham, M. (1997) 'Discourse analysis of a theme in one successful case of brief psychodynamic-interpersonal psychotherapy', *Journal of Counseling Psychology, 44*: 232–44.

Maguire, G.P., Goldberg, D.P., Hobson, R.F., Margison, F.R., Moss, S. and O'Dowd, T. (1984) 'Evaluating the teaching of a method of psychotherapy', *British Journal of Psychiatry, 144*: 575–80.

Mair, M. (1989) *Between Psychology and Psychotherapy: A Poetics of Experience*. London & New York: Routledge.

Malan, D. (1979) *Individual Psychotherapy and the Science of Psychodynamics*. London: Butterworths.

Margison, F.R. (1991) 'Learning to listen: Teaching and supervising basic psychotherapeutic skills'. In J. Holmes (ed.), *Textbook of Psychotherapy in Psychiatric Practice*. London: Churchill Livingstone, pp. 165–81.

Margison, F.R. (1995). 'Psychodynamic therapy'. In M. Jacobs (ed.), *Charlie an Unwanted Child: In Search of a Therapist*. Milton Keynes: Open University Press, pp. 68–87.

Margison, F.R. (1999) 'Psychotherapy: Advances in training methods', *Advances in Psychiatric Treatment, 5*: 329–37.

Margison, F.R. (2002) 'Psychodynamic-interpersonal psychotherapy'. In J. Holmes and A. Bateman (eds), *Integration in Psychotherapy: Models and Methods*. Oxford: Oxford University Press, pp. 107–24.

Margison, F.R., Barkham, M., Evans, C., McGrath, G., Mellor Clark, J., Audin, K. and Connell, J. (2000) 'Measurement and psychotherapy: Evidence-based practice and practice-based evidence', *British Journal of Psychiatry, 177*: 123–30.

Margison, F.R. and Moss, S. (1994) 'Teaching psychotherapy skills to inexperienced psychiatry trainees using the conversational model', *Psychotherapy Research, 4*: 141–8.

Martin, J. and Margison, F.R. (2000) 'The conversational model'. In S. Palmer and R. Woolfe (eds), *Integrative and Eclectic Counselling and Psychotherapy*. London: Sage, pp. 57–73.

Meares, R.A. (1977) *The Pursuit of Intimacy: An Approach to Psychotherapy*. Melbourne: Thomas Nelson.

Meares, R.A. (1993) *The Metaphor of Play: Origin and Breakdown of Personal Being*. Hove: Routledge.

Meares, R.A. (2000) *Intimacy and Alienation: Memory, Trauma and Personal Being*. London: Routledge.

Meares, R.A. (2012a). *Borderline Personality Disorder and the Conversational Model: A Clinician's Manual*. London: Norton.

Meares, R.A. (2012b) *A Dissociation Model of Borderline Personality Disorder*. London: Norton.

Meares, R.A. and Hobson, R.F. (1977) 'The persecutory therapist', *British Journal of Medical Psychology, 50*: 349–59.

Meares, R., Stevenson, J. and Comerford, A. (1999) 'Psychotherapy with borderline patients: A comparison between treated and untreated cohorts', *Australian and New Zealand Journal of Psychiatry, 33*: 467–72.

Mergenthaler, E. and Stinson, C. (1992) 'Psychotherapy transcription standards', *Psychotherapy Research, 2:* 125–42.

Milne, D.L., Baker, C., Blackburn, I.M., James, I.A. and Reichelt, F.K. (1999) 'Effectiveness of cognitive therapy training', *Journal of Behavior Therapy and Experimental Psychiatry, 30*, 81–92.

Moorey J. and Guthrie E. (2003) 'Persons and experience: Essential aspects of psycho-dynamic interpersonal therapy', *Psychodynamic Practice, 9*: 547–64.

Morrison, L.A. and Shapiro, D.A. (1987) 'Expectancy and outcome in prescriptive vs. exploratory psychotherapy', *British Journal of Clinical Psychology, 26*: 59–60.

Moss, S., Margison, F.R. and Godbert, K. (1991) 'The maintenance of psychotherapy skill acquisition: A two-year follow-up', *British Journal of Medical Psychology, 64*: 233–6.

NHS Confederation. (2009) 'Mental health work briefing', *Healthy Mind, Healthy Body, 179*: 1–6.

Paley, G., Cahill, J., Barkham, M., Shapiro, D.A., Jones, J., Patrick, S. and Reid, E. (2008) 'The effectiveness of psychodynamic-interpersonal therapy (PIT) in routine clinical practice: A benchmarking comparison', *Psychology and Psychotherapy: Theory, Research and Practice, 81*: 157–75.

Paley, G., Myers, J., Patrick, S. and Shapiro, D.A. (2003a) 'Practice development in psychological interventions: Mental health nurse involvement in the Conversational Model of psychotherapy', *Journal of Psychiatric Mental Health Nursing, 10*: 494–8.

Paley, G., Shapiro, D.A., Myers, J., Patrick, S. and Reid, E. (2003b) 'Personal reflections of mental health nurses training to use Hobson's Conversational Model (psychody-namic-interpersonal) of psychotherapy', *Journal of Psychiatric Mental Health Nursing, 10*: 735–42.

Palmieri, G., Margison, F.R., Guthrie, E., Moorey, J., Hardy, G.E., Evans, C., Barkham, M. and Rigatelli, M. (2007) 'A preliminary study of role-play competence in psychodynamic-interpersonal therapy', *Psychology and Psychotherapy, 80*: 327–31.

Paxton, R., Rhodes, D. and Crooks, I. (1988) 'Teaching nurses therapeutic conversation: A pilot study', *Journal of Advanced Nursing, 3*: 401–4.

Pistrang, N. and Barker, C. (1992) 'Clients' beliefs about psychological problems', *Counselling Psychology Quarterly, 5*: 325–36.

Raue, P.J., Goldfried, M.R. and Barkham, M. (1997) 'The therapeutic alliance in psy-chodynamic-interpersonal and cognitive-behavioral therapy', *Journal of Consulting and Clinical Psychology, 65*: 582–7.

Rees, A., Hardy, G.E., Barkham, M., Elliott, R., Smith, J. and Reynolds, S. (2001) '"It's like catching a desire before it flies away": A comprehensive analysis of a problem clarification event in cognitive-behavioral therapy for depression', *Psychotherapy Research, 11*: 331–51.

Reynolds, S., Stiles, W.B., Barkham B., Shapiro, D.A., Hardy, G.E. and Rees, A. (1996) 'Acceleration of changes in session impact during contrasting time limited psychother-apies', *Journal of Consulting and Clinical Psychology, 64*: 577–86.

Rogers, C. R. (1951) *Client Centred Therapy.* London: Constable.

Rudkin, A., Llewelyn, S., Hardy, G E., Stiles, W.B. and Barkham, M. (2007) 'Therapist and client processes affecting assimilation and outcome in brief psychotherapy', *Psychotherapy Research, 17*: 613–21.

Ryle, A. (1990) *Cognitive Analytic Therapy: Active Participation in Change.* Chichester: John Wiley.

Ryle, A. and Kerr, I. (2002) *Introducing Cognitive Analytic Therapy: Principles and Practice.* London: Wiley.

Sattel, H., Lahmann, C., Gündel, H., Guthrie, E., Kruse, J., Noll-Hussong, M., Ohmann, C., Ronel, J., Sack, M., Sauer, N., Schneider, G. and Henningsen P. (2012) 'Brief psy-chodynamic interpersonal psychotherapy for patients with multisomatoform disorder: randomised controlled trial', *British Journal of Psychiatry, 200*: 60–7.

Saxon, D. and Barkham, M. (2012) 'Patterns of therapist variability: Therapist effects and the contribution of patient severity and risk', *Journal of Consulting and Clinical Psychology, 80*: 535–46.

Schaefert, R., Kaufmann, C., Wild, B., Schellberg, D., Boelter, R., Faber, R., Szecsenyi, J., Sauer, N., Guthrie, E. and Herzog, W. (2013) 'Specific collaborative group intervention for patients with medically unexplained symptoms in general practice: a cluster randomised controlled trial', *Psychotherapy and Psychosomatics, 82*: 106–19.

Shapiro, D.A., Barkham, M., Rees, A., Hardy, G.E, Reynolds, S. and Startup, M. (1994) 'Effects of treatment duration and severity of depression on the effectiveness of cognitive-behavioural and psychodynamic-interpersonal psychotherapy', *Journal of Consulting and Clinical Psychology, 62*: 522–34.

Shapiro, D.A., Barkham, M., Reynolds, S.A., Hardy, G.E. and Stiles, W.B. (1992) 'Prescriptive and exploratory psychotherapies: Toward an integration based on the assimilation model'. *Journal of Psychotherapy Integration, 2*: 253–72.

Shapiro D.A., Barkham, M., Stiles, W.B., Hardy, G.E., Rees, A., Reynolds, S. and Startup, M. (2003) 'Time is of the essence: A selective review of the fall and rise of brief therapy research', *Psychology and Psychotherapy, 76*: 211–35.

Shapiro, D.A. and Firth, J. (1987) 'Prescriptive vs. exploratory psychotherapy: Outcomes of the Sheffield Psychotherapy Project', *British Journal of Psychiatry, 151*: 790–9.

Shapiro, D.A. and Firth-Cozens, J. (1990) 'Two-year follow-up of the Sheffield Psychotherapy Project', *British Journal of Psychiatry, 157*: 389–91.

Shapiro, D.A., Firth-Cozens, J. and Stiles, W.B. (1989) '"The question of therapists' differential effectiveness". A Sheffield Psychotherapy Project addendum', *British Journal of Psychiatry, 154*: 383–5.

Shapiro, D.A., Rees, A., Barkham, M. and Hardy, G.E. (1995) 'Effects of treatment duration and severity of depression on the maintenance of gains after cognitive-behavioral and psychodynamic-interpersonal psychotherapy', *Journal of Consulting and Clinical Psychology, 63*: 378–87.

Shapiro, D.A. and Shapiro, D. (1982) 'Meta-analysis of comparative therapy outcome studies: a replication and refinement', *Psychological Bulletin, 92*: 581–604.

Shapiro, D.A. and Startup, M.J. (1992) 'Measuring therapies adherence in Exploratory Psychotherapy', *Psychotherapy Research, 2*: 193–203.

Shaw, C.M., Margison, F.R., Guthrie, E. and Tomenson, B. (2001) 'Psychodynamic interpersonal therapy by inexperienced therapists in a naturalistic setting: A pilot study', *European Journal of Psychotherapy, Counselling and Health, 4:* 87–101.

Startup, M. and Shapiro, D.A. (1993) 'Therapist treatment fidelity in prescriptive vs. exploratory therapy', *British Journal of Clinical Psychology, 32*: 443–56.

Stern, D. (1985) *The Interpersonal World of the Infant: View from Psychoanalysis and Developmental Psychology.* New York: Basic Books.

Stevenson, J. and Meares, R. (1992) 'An outcome of psychotherapy for patients with borderline personality disorder', *American Journal of Psychiatry, 149*: 358–62.

Stiles, W.B. (1980) 'Measurement of the impact of psychotherapy sessions', *Journal of Consulting and Clinical Psychology, 48*: 176–85.

Stiles, W.B. (2002) 'Assimilation of problematic experiences'. In J.C. Norcross (ed.), *Psychotherapy Relationships That Work: Therapist Contributions and Responsiveness to Clients.* New York: Oxford University Press, pp. 165–81.

Stiles, W.B., Agnew-Davies, R., Hardy, G.E., Barkham, M. and Shapiro, D.A. (1998a) 'Relations of the alliance with psychotherapy outcome: Findings in the Second Sheffield Psychotherapy Project', *Journal of Consulting and Clinical Psychology, 66:* 791–802.

Stiles, W.B., Barkham, M., Shapiro, D.A. and Firth-Cozens, J. (1992) 'Treatment order and thematic continuity between contrasting psychotherapies: Exploring an implication of the assimilation model', *Psychotherapy Research, 2*: 112–24.

Stiles, W.B., Elliott, R., Llewelyn, S.P., Firth-Cozens, J.A., Margison, F.R., Shapiro, D.A. and Hardy, G.E. (1990) 'Assimilation of problematic experiences by client in psychotherapy', *Psychotherapy, 27*: 411–20.

Stiles, W.B., Glick, M.J., Osatuke, K., Hardy, G.E., Shapiro, D.A., Agnew-Davies, R., Rees, A. and Barkham, M. (2004a) 'Patterns of alliance development and the rupture-repair hypothesis: Are productive relationships U-shaped or V-shaped?', *Journal of Counseling Psychology, 51*: 81–92.

Stiles, W.B., Honos-Webb, L. and Surko, M. (1998b) 'Responsiveness in psychotherapy', *Clinical Psychology: Science and Practice, 5*: 439–58.

Stiles, W.B., Leiman, M., Shapiro, D.A., Hardy, G.E., Barkham, M., Detert, N.B. and Llewelyn, S.P. (2006) 'What does the first exchange tell? Dialogical sequence analysis and assimilation in very brief therapy', *Psychotherapy Research, 16*: 408–21.

Stiles, W.B., Morrison, L.A., Haw, S.K., Harper. H., Shapiro, D.A. and Firth-Cozens, J.A. (1991) 'Longitudinal study of assimilation in exploratory psychotherapy', *Psychotherapy, 28*: 195–206.

Stiles, W.B., Osatuke, K., Glick, M.J. and Mackay, H.C. (2004b) 'Encounters between internal voices generate emotion: An elaboration of the assimilation model'. In H.H. Hermans and G. Dimaggio (eds), *The Dialogical Self in Psychotherapy*. New York: Brunner-Routledge, pp. 91–107.

Stiles, W.B., Reynolds, S., Hardy, G.E., Rees, A., Barkham, M. and Shapiro, D.A. (1994) 'Evaluation and description of psychotherapy sessions by clients using the Session Evaluation Questionnaire and the Session Impacts Scale', *Journal of Counseling Psychology, 41*: 175–85.

Stiles, W.B., Shankland, M., Wright, J. and Field, S. (1997) 'Aptitude–treatment interactions based on clients' assimilation of their presenting problems', *Journal of Consulting and Clinical Psychology, 65*: 889–93.

Stiles, W.B. and Shapiro, D.A. (1995) 'Verbal exchange structure of brief psychodynamic-interpersonal and cognitive-behavioral psychotherapy', *Journal of Consulting and Clinical Psychology, 63*: 15–27.

Stiles, W.B., Shapiro, D.A. and Firth-Cozens, J.A. (1988) 'Verbal response mode use in contrasting psychotherapies: A within-subjects comparison', *Journal of Consulting and Clinical Psychology, 56*: 727–33.

Stiles, W.B., Shapiro, D.A. and Firth-Cozens, J.A. (1989) 'Therapist differences in the use of verbal response mode forms and intents', *Psychotherapy, 26*: 314–22.

Stiles, W.B., Startup, M., Hardy, G.E., Barkham, M., Rees, A., Shapiro, D.A. and Reynolds, S. (1996) 'Therapist session intentions in cognitive-behavioral and psychodynamic-interpersonal psychotherapy', *Journal of Counseling Psychology, 87*: 43–60.

Sullivan, H.S. (1940) *Conceptions of Modern Psychiatry*. New York: Norton.

Sullivan, H.S. (1953) *The Interpersonal Theory of Psychiatry*. New York: Norton.

Waltz, J., Addis, M.E., Koerner, K. and Jacobson, N.S. (1993) 'Testing the integrity of a psychotherapy protocol: Assessment of adherence and competence', *Journal of Consulting and Clinical Psychology, 61*: 620–30.

Zonzi, A., Barkham, M., Hardy, G.E., Llewelyn, S.P., Stiles, W.B. and Leiman, M. (2014) 'Zone of proximal development (ZPD) as an ability to play in psychotherapy: A theory-building case study of very brief therapy', *Psychology and Psychotherapy: Theory, Research and Practice, 87*: 447–64.

Index